Finding Our Way
TOGETHER

Bible Study Handbook
Book 1

For leaders of house groups

INTERNATIONAL BIBLE READING ASSOCIATION

Cover photograph – 'Look at this! Can you read this? We learn together.'
2nd Mile Bi-lingual Project, Bolivia – Sarah Bruce

Editor – Maureen Edwards

Published by:
The International Bible Reading Association
1020 Bristol Road
Selly Oak
Birmingham
Great Britain
B29 6LB

ISBN 0–7197–0897–4
ISSN 140–8593

© 1997 International Bible Reading Association

All rights reserved. No part of this publication may be reproduced, stored in a retrieval system, or transmitted, in any form or by any means, electronic, mechanical, photocopying, recording or otherwise, without the prior permission of the International Bible Reading Association.

Typeset by Avonset, Monmouth Place, Bath BA1 2NH
Printed and bound by Biddles Ltd., Guildford, Surrey

CONTENTS

	Page
The Writers	4
Acknowledgements	5
Useful addresses	5
How to use this book	6
Prayers	9
The Open Book (4 weeks)	16
Jesus – Man of mystery (3 weeks)	24
Lent and Passiontide (7 weeks)	30
Easter – He is risen indeed! (3 weeks)	44
Quality of life (3 weeks)	50
Pentecost – Filled by the Holy Spirit (2 weeks)	56
Personalities of the Bible (5 weeks)	60
Called to lead (2 weeks)	69
The power of prayer (2 weeks)	74
The Kingdom is for children (2 weeks)	79
Making sense of life (2 weeks)	84
Examine me, O God (2 weeks)	89
Blessed are the poor? (2 weeks)	93
Human rights (1 week)	100
God's shalom (3 weeks)	103
Oneness in Christ (2 weeks)	111
Christ comes in the flesh (2 weeks)	116
Advent (3 weeks)	121

THE WRITERS

Jane Ashplant A minister at Redhill who is a member of the Executive Committee of the Methodist Church Music Society.

Edmund Banyard A former Moderator of the United Reformed Church who now edits *All Year Round* for the Council of Churches for Britain and Ireland.

Philip Barker Methodist minister and former theme-writer for *Partners in Learning*.

Magali do Nascimento Cunha A young Brazilian journalist working with Koinonia, an ecumenical organization in Rio de Janeiro.

Penny Fowler Administrator of the Wesley and Methodist Studies Centre at Westminster College, Oxford.

Alec Gilmore Associate Baptist Chaplain in the Universities of Brighton and Sussex and Chairman of the IBRA Committee.

John Hastings A presbyter of the Church of North India and Bangladesh, well-known for his involvement in development and human rights.

Brian Haymes Principal of the Bristol Baptist College and author of IBRA's *Looking At ...* series.

Donald Hilton A former Moderator of the United Reformed Church who has written and compiled many books for NCEC.

Eileen Jacob A member of the Church of South India, who taught in a city grammar school in Hyderabad, and was superintendent of a village hostel.

Keith Johnson served on the UK Council of Amnesty International for six years and currently chairs its Religious Bodies Liaison Panel and the East Shropshire Group.

Melvyn Matthews Anglican priest and writer of a number of books on prayer and spirituality.

Joy Mead A poet and writer who is involved in justice and peace work.

Simon Oxley Executive Secretary for Education at the World Council of Churches in Geneva, Switzerland.

John R Pritchard A Methodist minister who has been involved for many years in world mission and international Church partnerships.

Helen Richmond A minister of the United Church of Aotearoa New Zealand, now teaching at the United College of the Ascension, Selly Oak, Birmingham.

Frances Shaw who teaches the Gospels section of the Guildford Diocesan Ministry Course, is involved in the work of Christian literacy, and is a member of the IBRA Committee.

Rosemary Wass A mother, farmer, local preacher, and a member of the IBRA Committee.

Acknowledgements

The editor and publisher express thanks for permission to use copyright items. Every effort has been made to trace copyright owners, but if any rights have been inadvertently overlooked, the necessary amendments will be made in subsequent editions.

For some of the graphic drawings we thank:

The Methodist Church (page 68) and the Nanjing Theological Seminary, China (pages 19, 40, 80 and 126)

Useful addresses

Amnesty International (British Section): 99-119 Rosebury Avenue, London EC1R 4RE

Catholic Fund for Overseas Development (CAFOD): 2 Romero Close, Stockwell Road, London SW9 9TY

Christian Aid, One World Week and the Council of Churches of Britain and Ireland (CCBI): Inter Church House, 35-41 Lower Marsh, London SE1 7RL

Commonwealth Institute: Kensington High Street, London W8 6NQ

Oxfam: 274 Banbury Road, Oxford OX2 2DZ

World Council of Churches: 150 Route de Ferney, 1211 Geneva 2, Switzerland

World Federation of the United Nations Association (UNA): The Pavilion du Petit Caconnex, 16 Avenue Jean Trembley, Geneva, Switzerland

How to use this book

Select
This book contains a variety of studies from which to select fresh themes. You do not have to start at the beginning and work through unless you choose to do so. There is enough material for 50 weeks of the year, but most groups meet only once a fortnight. Select
- what meets the needs of your group
- new topics which will challenge you
- themes which link with your church's programme and/or current concerns.

Adapt
Although we hope you will want to attempt new methods and ideas, feel free to adapt these studies to suit the needs of your group. Don't worry if there isn't time to try each exercise and discuss every question. Decide what can be omitted, and what you may want to add.

Prepare
Thorough preparation pays dividends. If you have a good grasp of the subject matter, you will feel more confident and more relaxed. Use a Bible commentary if necessary. The background notes in IBRA's *Words for Today 1998* and *Light for our Path 1998* (on the same themes) are helpful too. Ask yourself what questions are likely to arise, and how you will help the group to explore them. Remember – many questions are open-ended; there are no clear answers.

Act
Each theme includes a suggestion for action. You will not be able to try them all, but do try some. Otherwise the house group becomes an end in itself.

Pray
Pray that what you have prepared may be used by the Spirit to lead others to grow in faith. Make prayer a special feature of your house group. Begin with prayer and set aside time to share concerns and draw together the insights and challenges which come from the study. Support one another. As leader, pray for each member of your group.

Reflect
What did you achieve? What was difficult? Was it easier than you thought? If it went wrong, explore the reasons. What follow-up is necessary? What have you learned from the experience? Reflect on what you have done.

For regular IBRA readers
Groups who use IBRA's daily Bible reading notes in *Words for Today* and *Light for our Path* may want to cover as many themes as possible and integrate their meetings with personal study, as they have done in the past.

What next?
Look out for the next book in this series (available from autumn 1998). Topics for Book 2 are as follows:
1. God's World – God's Mission *(7 weeks)*
2. LENT – Encounters with Jesus *(7 weeks)*
3. New beginnings *(8 weeks)*
4. Sinai – Holy Land – Ephesus – Rome *(4 weeks)*
5. Forgive our debts – Jubilee 2000 *(2 weeks)*
6. Parables *(3 weeks)*
7. Personalities of the Bible *(6 weeks)*
8. Pilgrimage *(4 weeks)*
9. Questions of belief and practice *(7 weeks)*
10. Hope for the world *(5 weeks)*

A good leader is a good listener

What makes a good group leader?

A good leader

- helps the group to feel at ease and doesn't let the meeting drag on when everyone is waiting to go home,
- is sensitive to others' expectations,
- is a good listener, who learns from the group as well as leads,
- does not allow any member of the group to monopolize the discussion,
- does not force a quiet person to offer an opinion,
- can accept criticism,
- is not afraid to admit when s/he doesn't know the answer, but is willing to spend time exploring and finding out,
- will challenge the group when necessary,
- will enable and encourage others to share the leadership,
- is willing to try different methods,
- cares for the group and builds good relationships,
- has a sense of humour ...

Acknowledgements

NEB – *New English Bible* © Oxford University Press and Cambridge University Press 1961, 1970.

NIV – *New International Version* Copyright © 1973, 1978, 1984 by International Bible Society. Used by permission of Hodder & Stoughton Limited. All rights reserved.

NRSV – *New Revised Standard Version* © 1989, Division of Christian Education of the National Council of the Churches of Christ in the USA.

RSV – *The Holy Bible, Revised Standard Version* © 1973, Division of the National Council of Churches of Christ in the USA.

PRAYERS AND MEDITATIONS

An opening prayer
Loving God,
in quietness, we feel your presence
and in wonder, we greet you in each other.
Creator of all things,
who made each of us different,
we thank you that you have drawn us together as a group
to explore the meaning of your Word for today.
Increase in us your gift of humility
that we may be open to new thoughts
and follow where your Spirit leads.
Strengthen our faith that we may not back away
when the questions disturb us
and we are challenged to think and act in new ways.

Be with us,
and may your presence cleanse our lives.
Be with us,
and may your love redeem us.
Be with us,
and may your Spirit make us one. Amen

A closing prayer
Gracious God, we commit ourselves to you.
Come into our lives.
Fill us with your light, wisdom, grace and love,
so that your transforming power
may work in us and make us one with you
and your will for the world and all its people.
Bless us as we go
and as we seek to live by the thoughts we have shared.

God who gave us life, enfold us in your love.
God in Christ, forgive our past.
God the Holy Spirit, disturb and change our ways
and lead us on. Amen

Thanksgiving

Lord, your glory fills the world
and is seen in the life and work of all people.
You are present in the experience
and cultural heritage of all races.
You inspire our use of colour, sound and movement
and the rich resources of the earth.
You made us in your image
and gave us your creative ability.
Thank you, Creator and Provider of all.

Thank you for gifts of communication,
speech and language;
for the art of storytelling,
enabling us to pass on traditions
from one generation to another;
for the gift of writing
and the enrichment of mind
that comes from the literature,
poetry and wise sayings
of people of many countries and periods of history.
Thank you, Creator and Provider of all.

Thank you for the gift of dramatic art,
the development of radio and television
and the wealth of talent from many cultures
they bring into our homes.
Thank you, Creator and Provider of all.

Thank you for varieties of sound and rhythm
and the power of music and dance
to make us forget ourselves
and become one with the community.
Thank you, Creator and Provider of all.

Thank you for works of art and architecture,
woodcarvings and sculpture,
beautiful jewellery and ornaments,
and the fashioning and design
of clothes and textiles.
Thank you, Creator and Provider of all.

Thank you for the gift of knowledge
and the development of science;
that we can look through microscopes
at the smallest units of your creation
and discover wonders invisible to the naked human eye;
for the use of radiation
in the diagnosis and treatment of disease;
for new methods of agriculture
to combat soil erosion,
cultivate deserts
and provide food for everyone.
Thank you, Creator and Provider of all.

Confession

Loving God,
day by day you reveal to us your purity and love,
and we long to be like you.
You speak to us through your Word
and call us back to love you with our whole being,
but we respond by offering only a small part of our lives.

In Christ, you showed us how to put ourselves last,
but we go on being self-centred and insensitive
to the needs and expectations
of people around us.
In the death of Christ, you suffered for our redemption,
but we turn back again and again
to the ways from which you set us free.

Forgive us, heal us,
and love us into a deeper devotion to you
and faithfulness to the ways of your Kingdom.
In the name of Christ. Amen

For peace

Loving God, like dry land waiting for rain,
we long for the peace Christ offers:
creative peace, forming one new community in himself,
not silent acquiescence which allows evil to flourish,
but peace breaking down walls of separation, hatred and pride,
healing all relationships
and enabling us to grow through
mutual trust and understanding
and by an unconditional, unlimited forgiveness of one another.

May we go in peace
like the woman who touched the hem of his garment,
healed to enjoy unbroken unity with you,
and to share in your mission to create harmony
within our families, communities and all creation.

For openness

Jesus spoke in parables – simple, vivid stories.
People enjoyed them but went away
because they did not want to commit themselves
to 'go and do likewise'.
They did not want to be released
from the mould of their set ways.
Their minds were closed to new truths.
They could not begin to understand or change.
The deeper meaning of the parable was hidden.
His commands – to love their enemies,
to forgive one another,
to live alongside and accept as partners people of all races,
to give and make all that they had available for others to share,
to believe that the meek will inherit the earth –
were foolishness to them.

Lord Jesus Christ, set us free from attitudes
that block the activity of your Spirit within us.
Open our minds and hearts daily to receive your truth.
Help us to see the challenges and opportunities
to which we are blind.

For refugees

We pray for refugees,
driven from their towns and villages by political turmoil,
children whose homes have been destroyed,
asylum-seekers rejected
and deported from a country of refuge,
migrants separated from their families.
They knock at our door.
Loving God, who came as a stranger,
unacknowledged, pushed out by society
to die on a cross as a criminal,
you come into our country as a stranger,
challenging us to discover
what it means to be your children.
Give us grace to speak out
and act on behalf of the powerless
that we may not close the door on you.
Based on the Christmas message of the World Council of Churches 1996

For our towns and cities

Loving God, we rejoice with you
in the achievements of our towns and cities,
their architecture, industries and culture –
signs of vitality and opportunity.
We also weep with you at the widening gap
between rich and poor:
busy people overwhelmed by stress,
traffic congestion and pollution,
unemployed, homeless young people in Britain,
street children in Brazil,
women and men, isolated and forgotten,
crucified peoples ...
Yet there you are; you share the pain,
and pierce the darkness with light and hope,
challenging the world from the margins.
Through the words of the poor,
you offer redeeming grace to fill
and inspire us to wait upon and serve one another,
so that our polluted urban life may be transformed
into cities whose builder and maker is God.

Forgive our debts

'Forgive our debts as we forgive ...'
Forgive our preoccupation with our own interests
and slowness to see the needs of others.
Forgive our unwillingness
to risk unpopularity and speak out,
our reluctance to forgive debts owing to us.
Fill us with joy to proclaim in word and deed,
the Year of Jubilee, release for prisoners of conscience
and remission of debts for the poorest nations.

Signs of the Kingdom – a meditation

Give us a sign, we ask:
miracles of healing and mass conversions.
Yet more often Christ is present in the few:
women and men serving wholeheartedly in depressing
    situations.
His voice surprises and challenges us
through people of other faiths
whose love for God and their neighbours
shines out in all they do;
through young people,
frustrated by the inflexibility of older generations,
who challenge Christians to stand against evil.
He comes from the margins –
a victim of AIDS, a drug addict, the prisoner, the hungry,
a person with disabilities –
challenging our worldly values.
When we talk of money and status,
he talks of serving with empty hands: 'Sell ... Give ...'
Who are the great? They are the meek,
ordinary people who wash one another's feet.
What is the Kingdom like?
It is not like any world power;
it is like yeast, cells within society,
breaking, exploding, disturbing, influencing others
and, like the sign of Jonah which Jesus promised,
changing communities.

God is light – a meditation

Shafts of light appear over the horizon,
across vast plains,
filtering through valleys, like the first dawn,
setting a contrast for silhouettes of rocks and trees,
piercing darkness with suffused rays,
giving way to deeper, richer tones
as the sun – reflected in the sparkle of dewdrops,
waves and ripples of streams,
rivers and oceans – fills the day with radiance.
All is fresh and cool,
with sounds of waking,
the resumed activity of birds and insects,
chickens and animals, people and traffic,
bringing certainty, confidence and vision
through the light God gives.

Light and life are one.
Throughout the night,
lights of fishing vessels
move against the blackness of sea and sky,
in and out of the harbour,
and on land, in the lights of homes, factories and hospitals,
illuminations in city streets,
and the headlights of cars and buses
declare their defiance of darkness.

Out of chaos, God gave light.
God is light,
the full majesty and brilliance of dazzling crystal,
giving birth to all colours of the rainbow,
cascading into and disturbing preferred darkness,
piercing with hope
all who cry out for deliverance from pain,
who long for the earth to be filled
with the light of God's love
as it was revealed in Jesus Christ.

The prayers and meditations on pages 9–15 are by the editor:
© Maureen Edwards.

NOTES
BY
ROSEMARY WASS

THE OPEN BOOK

In 1998 in England, the Churches are seeking to encourage more people to read and study the Bible. This movement from *Churches Together* – called 'The Open Book' – is partly a response to the Pope's challenge to all Christians to prepare for the Millennium. Fully aware of our partnership with Churches in other parts of the world, it seeks 'to make the Bible culturally relevant to the different cultures in England'. In the first four studies of this book, we shall look together at some of the features which continue to make the Bible the world's best-seller.

Study 1 *Celebrate the stories*

Keynote readings
Genesis 2.4b-25
Genesis 12.1-9
Exodus 2.1-10
2 Samuel 12.1-14
Ruth 1.1-22
Matthew 2.1-12
John 4.7-42
Luke 10.25-37

AIM
To explore, enjoy and celebrate the richness of narrative in the Bible.

Preparation
1. *It will be helpful for the leader to prepare a comfortable atmosphere; lighting, hospitality, and the placing of the chairs so that every member of the group can have mutual eye contact, are important for this to happen.*
2. *Please have a supply of paper and pens available.*
3. *Before the meeting, the leader will need to think of a well-known Bible story and think carefully of the details that will remind others of it.*

Way in
Encourage members to think back to their childhood and focus on one incident, perhaps related to family life, or church life, or education, or even a dream, and then share it with another member of the group.
- Could we each relate to the other stories?
- Did it remind us of something else in our own lives?

Telling a story
1. Tell the group that you are going to begin to tell a

well-known Bible story, and invite others to continue its telling. You will need to sense when it will be appropriate to invite the group to reveal which story it is. The actual story may be discovered quickly, but continue the telling for the whole of it with as many participating as possible.

When the story has been told, invite members to locate (from memory) the narrative in the Bible, insisting on the precise location! Encourage everyone to sit and read the story quietly.
- How accurately was the story told?
- Do different versions of the Bible give a variety of emphases on the same narrative?
- Are there contemporary stories from our own culture which might complement the shared story? Do not be afraid to take time to think carefully about this, and then have a time of sharing.

2. Supply people with a sheet of paper and pen, and invite them to make a list of their favourite biblical stories. Share the lists by having one contribution per person and keep going round the group until all have been named.
- Was there a clear favourite?
- Why would that particular story have that honour?
- What are the special elements of this/these stories?
- What purposes do you think the writers of the stories had in telling them? E.g. to make a point, a surprise element, to help people relate, to make people think and come to decisions themselves, to disclose a truth, as a protest against what was happening ...

3. People may like to work in pairs and think of examples of specific categories of the narratives set for the week.
- What does this tell us about communication?
- Do you think that these forms of communication will continue to be as relevant for the next millennium?

PRAYER/REFLECTION

To close the session, the leader may invite another member of the group to read again the story they began with. Then have a time of quiet followed by open prayer celebrating the gift of vivid and helpful narrative that has stood the test of time.

Do you think that these forms of communication will continue to be as relevant for the next millennium?

17

Study 2 *Celebrate poetry*

Keynote readings
Psalm 23
Psalm 46
Psalm 103
Song of Songs 2.3-15
Job 19.21-27
Luke 1.46-55
Matthew 5.3-12

AIM
To celebrate the beauty of poetry through psalms and poems.

Preparation
Invite members to select a piece of poetry which is special to them, and a favourite psalm to share with the group.

The leader will chair this session to weave together the readings and thoughts of members, remembering that poetry is about concentrated word pictures and expression.

Introductory exercise
Encourage each group member to share an item of celebration during this past week: e.g. a birth, an award, a birthday, an anniversary, good news of some sort, even life itself.

The appeal and challenge of poetry
1. Agree an appropriate procedure for the meeting, e.g. to listen to one another's favourite poem, or hymn, and reasons the members wish to share.
2. You may choose to have a short break then, and/or a drink.
3. Then share your favourite psalms and poetry of the Bible, reading to one another the verses which mean most to you.
4. Finally read one of the passages given in the margin which has not already been chosen, and reflect on the insights which touch your experience.

ACTION
Choose one psalm to share within an act of worship the following Sunday and read it chorally with the congregation.

Conclude your meeting with the following poem:

The Sharing

We told our stories
That's all
We sat and listened to each other
And heard the journeys of each soul.
We sat in silence
Entering each one's pain and sharing each one's joy.
We heard love's longing and the lonely reaching-out
For love and affirmation.
We heard of dreams shattered. And visions fled.
Of hopes and laughter turned stale and dark.
We felt the pain of isolation and the bitterness of death.

But in each brave and lonely story
God's gentle life broke through ...
And we heard music in the darkness
And smelled flowers in the void.

We felt the budding of creation
In the searchings of each soul
And discerned the beauty of God's hand in
Each muddy, twisted path.

And God sang in each story
God's life sprang from each death.
Our sharing became one story of a
    simple lonely search
For life and hope and oneness
In a world which sobs for love.
And we knew that in our sharing
God's voice with mighty breath
Was saying ...
Love each other and take each
    other's hand.

For you are one though many
And in each of you I live.
So listen to my story and share my
    pain and death
Oh, listen to my story
And rise and live with me.

From There Was No Path So I Trod One by Edwina Gateley
(published by Source Books, California, USA)

Study 3 *Celebrate history*

Keynote readings
Exodus 14.10-31
2 Samuel 5.1-12
1 Kings 6.1-14
John 1.1-14

AIM

To celebrate our Christian history and historic events within our own lifetime.

Preparation

Encourage group members to spend some time looking at old diaries and/or photographs they may have, or to reflect on significant points of history in their own lives. Some members may have Family Trees or Family Bibles which they might like to bring and share with the group.

Changes all around us

In pairs,
- reflect on important personal historical events, sharing from the diaries and family albums you have brought;
- think of important advances which are now history, even within our lifetime, e.g. computer technology and the impact on communications, transport, household aids, electrical equipment and forms of heating in our homes, medicine and longer life expectancy in many parts of the world, space travel and environmental implications ...

Biblical reflection

Divide into pairs and ask each pair to read one of the passages given in the margin. Together as a group share with one another the changes which would have come about as a result of each of the significant moments in history which are described.
- How important is it to understand our history?
- How far is it 'our story'?

Changes in the life of the Church

Encourage members to think of the historical advances of the Church within our respective denominations and ecumenically, trying to keep the emphasis on celebration. E.g. the place of women in the Church (1998 marks the close of *The Decade of Churches In Solidarity With Women*), social outreach, the Missionary Movement, the understanding of ministry within the Church and the relationship of lay and ordained ministries ...

- Has the Church kept pace with the world's changes, e.g. in music, liturgy, participation etc.?
- What are the most exciting and important pieces of history for members of the group?
- How significant will the dawning of the Millennium be to us all?
- How should the Church mark its coming?
- Will this be written into the history books for future generations?

PRAYER/REFLECTION

1. To bring the session to a close, light a candle as a focus and encourage members to think of individuals who have been a source of encouragement/introduction/nurture to them in their Christian pilgrimage. Following the opportunity for sharing, move into a time of open prayer celebrating the lives of those whose names are part of our personal histories.
2. Close with the sharing of the Peace, reminding each other of the historical context in which Jesus promised peace to his friends and disciples.

How significant will the dawning of the Millennium be to us all?

Study 4 *Celebrate God's love*

AIM
To take more time to think of and celebrate God's love for each of us.

Keynote readings
Hosea 11.1-4, 8-9
Isaiah 49.13-16
John 3.1-17
Romans 8.31-39
Deuteronomy 6.4-9
Mark 12.28-34
1 Corinthians 13.1-13

Preparation
You will need a Love-feast cup (or suitable alternative) and a jug of water.

Begin the session with an informal arrangement of chairs, and then, for the Agape move the chairs into a circle, with the jug and loving cup on a table in the centre.

The love of God
Begin the session by inviting reflection on the 'celebrations' so far. Think of shared stories, poetry and history. Read together Hosea 11.1-4, 8-9; Isaiah 49.13-16; and John 3.1-17 and reflect on the meaning of these words in your lives.
- Do we take God's love for granted?

Do we take God's love for granted?

21

- Have the keynote readings this week heightened our awareness of God's love?
- Invite members to share the reading of Psalm 139 and to think of the assurance of God's love within it.

Agape – Love-feast

Now issue an invitation for members to participate in an *Agape*, a Love-feast, celebrating God's love for each of us. It is important to assure people that this is neither Holy Communion nor a substitute for it. It is a reflection of God's love for us, and thus our love for God and other people. The *Agape* stems from Jesus' summary of the law and the prophets by the double commandment: 'Love the Lord your God with all your heart, with all your soul, and with all your mind', and 'Love your neighbour as yourself'.

Arrange the chairs in a circle with the water and container in the centre. If possible play some quiet music, or have a time of quietness.

The cup of water is passed from one person to the other. A Love-feast cup usually has a handle on each side, so that the cup can be passed easily from one hand to another. As the person holds the cup, s/he takes time to share his/her experience of God's love *(this should be unhurried with room for silence between each contribution).*

You may like to suggest a phrase with which the contribution can be brought to a close, such as 'For the gift of this love to me', so that all can respond with 'Thanks be to God'. When the person has spoken, s/he takes a drink of the water, and then passes the cup to the next person, and so on around the circle.

PRAYER

To bring this celebration to a close:

The cup of water given for thee
   Still holds the freshness of thy grace;
Yet long these multitudes to see
   The strong compassion of thy face.

Frank Mason North (1850-1935)

BLESSING

Go in peace, go in love,
Finding joy in each other.
Go in peace, go in love,
In Christ we're sister and brother.
Led by His Spirit, there's strength each day.
Light for the way – together.
Go in peace, go in love.
May God be with us for ever. Amen
    From Celebrating Together (Corrymeela Press)
           8 Upper Crescent, Belfast BT17 1NT

And may God
be with us
for ever

WORDS FOR TODAY

- A rich, exciting collection of daily Bible readings for the year, exploring books of the Bible alongside contemporary themes

- A complimentary volume to *Light for our Path*

UK price £3.99

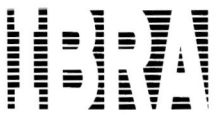

Order through your IBRA representative or from the appropriate address on page 128.

NOTES BY
BRIAN HAYMES

JESUS – MAN OF MYSTERY
Gospel of Mark 1-9

Study 1 *Keeping quiet about Jesus*

Keynote readings
Mark 1.1 to 3.12

AIM
To explore the theme of secrecy in Mark's Gospel.

Way in
Ask the group to read quietly the first three chapters of Mark's Gospel, noting the times Jesus asks the disciples, or people touched by his ministry, not to tell others about him. List the occasions on a flip chart, or large sheet of paper, for all to see.
- What reasons can you give for these requests for silence? *(For example, that Jesus did not want to be known simply as a healer, or exorcist).*
- What of the argument that Jesus could have exploited such fame by preaching to the crowds that would have gathered? Why not shout out the great things God is doing?
- Does the group see any lessons here for the Church's evangelism?

And could they keep quiet?
Again, ask the group to look at the stories and this time draw out the fact that in many cases the command to silence is utterly impossible to fulfil. How could the man with leprosy keep quiet?

The way to the cross
Some scholars have suggested that this impossibility means that the call for 'secrecy' is an editorial contribution from Mark. He faithfully records that Jesus did many wonderful works but he does not want his readers to jump to any superficial judgements about who Jesus really is. The miracles are important but they do not tell the whole story. For that, Mark must take his readers carefully to the

cross. It is only here that the truth is told completely. Notice how Mark's Gospel comes to a climax as the centurion confesses the faith that Jesus is the Son of God (15.39). Before the cross Mark records three 'passion predictions' from Jesus, at 8.31. 9.31 and 10.33-34. The cross and the suffering, which must have seemed so humiliating and impossible for the Son of God, in fact are the place where the true identity of Jesus is revealed. He is the one who suffers and gives his life as a 'ransom for many'.

- Do you find the death of Jesus on the cross an embarrassment, a puzzle or a revelation? Invite the group to discuss how they would help others to understand the significance of the fact that Jesus is the Son of God, not in spite of the fact that he suffers, but because he does.
- Think about the mission task of the Church. Many evangelistic campaigns look to use creative and attractive publicity and advertizing. What would an evangelistic ministry which focused on Mark's Gospel look like?

Do you find the death of Jesus on the cross an embarrassment, a puzzle or a revelation?

ACTION

Ask the group to look critically at their Church's local and national advertizing.
- What is the message that is coming across?
- Is it consistent with the Gospel of Jesus?
- How could it be improved?

PRAYER

Invite the group to prepare and use a prayer
1. of confession for the ways the Church distorts the gospel of Jesus,
2. of thanksgiving for the work of those in the ministry of healing today,
3. to ask for greater insight into who Jesus is and what he has done for us.

Study 2 *Parables and understanding*

Keynote readings
Mark 4.1 to 6.6

AIM
To explore the meaning and power of parables.

Way in
Ask the members of the group to recall their favourite parable of Jesus, and to say why it is their favourite. Let each member of the group share their views and then, when all have spoken, try to identify any common perceptions about parables. Why do parables hold our attention and stimulate our imagination?

The purpose of parables
Read Mark 4.1-9. Discuss the parable and what it means but keep the attention of the group on these verses only. What do people see and hear in the parable of the sower?

Then, read Mark 4.10-12. How is this saying of Jesus with its Old Testament quotation to be understood?

To the disciples, Jesus says that they have been given the 'secret'. This could mean either that in the hearing of the parables, and acting upon them, the disciples are sharing the Kingdom present in Jesus. It is secret only in the sense that it involves listening to and obeying Jesus. It is thus an 'open' secret. Or, it could simply mean that Jesus himself is the secret, present among his disciples. What of those on the 'outside'? Are they really told parables so that they do not perceive, understand and receive forgiveness? Sad to say, that was certainly the result of Jesus' teaching for some. Some scholars suggest that here is an illustration of an Aramaic form of speech whereby the result of something is described as its purpose. Jesus told parables to help people understand and turn to God. The result was that many did not. The sower cannot control the soil!

(The group leader may want to consult some commentaries before the meeting. The Pelican Gospel Commentary on Saint Mark by D E Nineham has some useful reflections on these verses).

Discovering meaning
Read Mark 4.13-20. Invite the group simply to hear one of its members read the story. Ask the others to put their

Bibles aside for the moment. Encourage the group to describe the scene in their imagination:
- What do they see? Feel?
- Are there particular moments in the story that touch them? Can they say why?
- What sort of soil are our lives? Let the group respond as openly and freely as it can to these verses.

Different contexts?
The image of the sower, while understandable, is not going to be common to all, especially to those who live in cities.
- Can the group suggest another image or way of picturing the message the group has discerned in the parable? Would the picture of a campaigning journalist do?
- Can the group begin to think of common situations, or observations, around which a parable might be composed?

Encouraging storytellers
Stories are what we remember. Should we encourage storytellers in the Church? How might this be done? *(Beware of stories that are really only moral or improving tales).* The best stories always fire up imaginations in such a way that hearers become part of the story and go on living in it. Remember how stories can frighten, or make us laugh, or prompt us to action.

Should we encourage storytellers in the Church?

Proclaiming the Gospel
Draw the discussion together by asking what these reflections might imply for the Church in its task of proclaiming the gospel. Think particularly what this might mean for preaching. Consider the importance of telling the local church's own story, warts and all. Or, perhaps, an older member of the group might like to reflect on his or her life story and with the group begin to reflect on its spiritual significance.

PRAYER
Focus the prayers on the ministry of preachers and teachers, the work of television, radio and newspaper journalists, the need for storytellers in the service of the gospel.

Study 3 *Following the mysterious Jesus*

Keynote readings
Mark 6.30 to 9.13

AIM
To reflect on the meaning of following the 'Man of mystery'.

Way in
Ask the group to imagine that they are responsible for designing a course for those who have enquired about the meaning of being a Christian disciple. On a flip-chart, or large piece of paper, write up all the suggested ideas for content.

Imagine that the first session is to be entitled 'Follow our leader' and that it is to begin with an exploration of who Jesus is and why he is to be followed. Ask the group to describe their own 'picture' of Jesus who is to be followed.

Biblical reflection
Then invite the group to examine the following passages – Mark 1.9-13; 1.21-28; 2.13-17; 3.31-35; 4.35-41; 6.1-5; 8.27-30. Divide the passages between members of the group and ask them to identify key descriptions of Jesus and words that are significant about him based on these passages. Write up these contributions on the chart.

Encourage the members to discuss the picture that emerges.
- How far do they feel comfortable with it?
- Has their original picture caught the strangeness of Jesus?
- Are there aspects of the picture Mark paints that are strange to their experience? Why do they think this is?
- What are the differences between the first personal picture painted of Jesus and that of Mark's?

What image of Jesus do we share with others?
- It has always been a serious temptation for the Church to make Jesus 'after our image'. It is evident from Mark's Gospel that many found Jesus a strange and difficult figure. Invite the group to suggest ways in which we can keep the picture of the strange but fascinating Jesus of the Gospels before us. What would they suggest as advice to a new disciple?

- In particular, notice how Jesus called people to 'follow' him. How can the Church be kept faithful to Jesus, and not simply following our own image of him?
- What does the group feel about the contrast between our emphasis on the Church as an institution – which grows, with professional staff, and that seeks a security for its own life – and the call of Jesus to carry the cross, to give one's life, even to lose it for the sake of the gospel?
- Is it possible that we have made Church membership too easy?
- In avoiding the radical strangeness of Jesus, have we altered the meaning not merely of discipleship but of the Gospel itself?

These are serious thoughts. Albert Schweitzer (in *Quest*) said that it was only in the following that we would know really who Jesus is:

'He comes to us as One unknown, without a name, as of old, by the lakeside, He came to those who knew him not. He speaks to us the same word: "Follow thou me!" and sets us to the tasks which He has to fulfil for our time. He commands. And to those who obey Him, whether they be wise or simple, He will reveal Himself in peace and work, in the toil and the pain they pass through in His fellowship, and, as an ineffable mystery, they shall learn in their own experience who He is.'

Is it possible that we have made Church membership too easy?

PRAYER

Begin with a time of silence when everyone can think about the call of Jesus to them as individuals and as a group.

Read Mark 8.31 to 9.1.

Then pray together:

Loving, gracious Lord Jesus,
you have called us to share your life and mission.
We admit that this scares us.
You ask much of us, but you gave all for us.
This is a strange love you give and go on giving,
unlimited and free.
We ask that you will strengthen us to live as your true disciples.
Help us to follow you faithfully. Amen

NOTES BY
JOHN HASTINGS (STUDY 1)
PHILIP BARKER (STUDIES 2 &3)
EDMUND BANYARD (STUDIES 4 & 5)
PENNY FOWLER (STUDIES 6 & 7)

Keynote readings
Isaiah 58.1-8
Mark 2.18-22
Luke 4.1-13
Matthew 6.1-6, 16-21
2 Corinthians 6.1-10

LENT AND PASSIONTIDE

Study 1   *True fasting*

AIM
To encourage one another to decide how a period of fasting (e.g. Lent, or to demonstrate a protest) can help us towards lives of greater self-discipline.

Preparation
Collect a few facts about any group which has fasted for a cause, to gain its own rights, or to express solidarity with victimized people and demand justice for them. Prepare to present the case for one particular fast. This could be presented as a role play.

Way in
Let each member of the group speak about his/her experience of fasting, and what benefits it has brought.

Discuss
- What are the pitfalls and what are the potential gains of ritual fasting?
- Do you think Jesus considered that the old Law was superseded by the new law of Love?
- Look at each of the keynote readings in the margin. How do they affect your attitude to fasting, especially Lenten discipline?
- Is Christian self-discipline a matter of copying Jesus? If so, how far? Would it mean becoming homeless and dependent on the hospitality of others?
- Do those of us who live in the West need help to avoid being sucked into a constant affluent lifestyle?
- Some of us enjoy modern comforts and facilities: what would Jesus' yardstick be for assessing their true value and accepting them?

Sharing life experience
Ask each member of the group in turn to tell of disciplines s/he has undergone for sport or work – study for an

examination, apprenticeship for a trade, assault courses in army training, leadership courses for responsible posts, jogging etc.
- Many organizations have rules for their members. What are the unwritten 'rules' for Christ's disciples today?
- As a sportsman trains for an event, are there appropriate disciplines which help us to follow the way of Christ?

Fasting in solidarity

Ask members of the group to share information about individuals, or groups who have fasted as an act of solidarity with others, or as a protest against injustice. Alternatively ask some of the members to present a role play.

After the presentation, discuss your immediate reactions, and share any other examples of fasting for one's own or others' rights.

Discuss and decide whether there are any current or potential issues for which you would be prepared to fast.

ACTION – REFLECTION – PRAYER

In small groups, write down some resolutions for your group's action towards a truer Christian lifestyle, to be achieved either as a Lenten discipline, or as a permanent undertaking.

Or ask individuals to write down their decisions about lifestyle. In this case it would be best that they remain private.

Place the paper/papers in a large metal, fireproof bowl and burn them, offering yourselves with your resolutions as a living sacrifice, and praying that you may practise self-discipline in some form every day, knowing Christ the Bridegroom is with you.

Are there appropriate disciplines which help us to follow the way of Christ?

Study 2 *Above all Christ!*

Keynote reading
Hebrews 2.5-18

AIM
To affirm Jesus and his teaching as the focus of our faith.

It helps to concentrate the mind!
If appropriate, follow up last week's session on *True Fasting*: what were the results of your decisions ?

Lent is an opportunity to focus on what really matters. It does help to concentrate the mind!

> 'If you are making plans for Lent, make sure you don't make them for the wrong reasons. Decide before God first what you'll do to amend your life, then what you can do during the coming weeks to help you towards that goal.'
> *John Hastings*
> *From Words for Today (IBRA 1998)*

A sharp focus
Read Hebrews 2.5-18 and note especially what verse 17 says about Jesus – 'For this reason he had to be made like his brothers in every way, in order that he might become a merciful and faithful high priest in service to God ...' (NIV)

> 'In Jesus we see the reality of the intended glory demonstrated, and its possibility remaining an offering of renewed hope. All this has been accomplished through a unique act of solidarity with us human beings displayed in Jesus ...'
> *Burchel Taylor*
> *From Words for Today (IBRA 1998)*

- How important is Jesus in our faith?
- Why does he matter so much?

> 'No believer can cope with adversity unless Christ fills his horizons, sharpens his priorities and dominates his experience.'
> *Raymond Brown in The Message of the Hebrews –*
> *The Bible Speaks Today series (IVP 1982)*

- Share personal experiences of Christ helping us cope with adversity.
- What are the priorities that Jesus challenges?

What are the priorities that Jesus challenges?

Study 4 *Peter*

AIM

To get to know the man behind the story so that Peter's experiences can help us in our own discipleship.

Keynote readings
Luke 5.1-11
Matthew 16.13-23
Mark 14.26-31
John 21.1-19
Acts 4.1-19
Acts 10.34-48
Galatians 2.6-14

Getting to know Peter

Either in pairs, or together as a group, recall all the stories of Peter in the New Testament and list his strengths on one side of a sheet of paper, and his weaknesses on the other. Take each point you have made, and identify and discuss the ways Jesus used both his strengths and weaknesses.

- What might Peter have learnt from the experiences (*of our last three weeks' studies*) of Elijah and Jeremiah?
- Which story of Peter means most to members of the group, and why?

Getting to know ourselves

Often others recognize our gifts and faults better than we can see ourselves. If we learn to welcome their insights it will help us to grow. It is important that we should make a correct assessment of ourselves (see Romans 12.3).

1. Ask the group to spend a moment in silence considering what they each recognize as their own strengths and weaknesses. If it helps, write them down.
2. Go around the group, ask each person to identify a **strength** which they see in the person sitting on their right. This can often surprise us, and is very affirming.
3. Then ask them in turn to admit to one **weakness**, or – if your members are used to being open to each other, you may be able to get them to identify one another's weaknesses.
   - How can these strengths, and even our weaknesses, enrich our common life and enable us to serve Christ in the world?
   - What can we learn from Peter's experience?
4. Read again Galatians 2.6-14.
   - What local issues might be dividing the group, or your church, or churches in the area?
   - How can difficult issues and challenges enable us to grow in faith and love of God?

How can difficult issues and challenges enable us to grow in faith and love of God?

If the exercise above brings out particular failures or experiences that cause depression, the group should be encouraged lovingly to minister forgiveness, acceptance and support in Christ's name. This will naturally lead into a time of prayer.

PRAYER

If possible, ask each person to volunteer to pray for another member of the group, ensuring that all are prayed for.

ACTION

Take an issue currently hitting the headlines or dominating conversations in your area, especially one in which the authorities have got it wrong. Discuss the issue for a while, and then ask what can be done about it. Work out a practical way in which the group can express its opinion and show concern. Try to ensure that your aim and proposed action are constructive.

Study 5   Lesser-known personalities

AIM

Keynote readings
Mark 15.21
Romans 16.13
Acts 4.36-37; 11.19-26
Acts 16.16-40

To identify with lesser-known people mentioned in the Bible and to discover ways in which God is using us, and which we may not have recognized.

Way in

Make a list of people you can remember who are only briefly referred to in the Bible. By each name add the task s/he performed.

Simon of Cyrene

Read Mark 15.21. This is all we are told about Simon. He came from Cyrene in North Africa, and African people today are proud to identify with one who carried the cross for Jesus. Why do you think Mark refers to Alexander and Rufus?

Read Romans 16.13. Could this be the same Rufus named by Mark? Is it possible that Simon's encounter with Jesus on the way to Golgotha led to his conversion? Certainly his sons later became members of the Church at Rome. Put together the story of Simon as far as you can see it and reflect on its significance.

● What challenges does it make to you?

Barnabas
The name means 'son of encouragement'. Read Acts 4.36-37; 9.27 and 11.19-26, and see how he lived out this meaning.

Other references to Barnabas are found in Acts 13 to 15. After helping to spread the faith in Antioch, he joined Paul at Tarsus where they worked together for a year. He went with Mark and Paul on their first mission to Asia Minor, and later helped Paul at the Council of Jerusalem to defend their work among the Gentiles. After that, Paul and Barnabas parted. Barnabas took John Mark, his cousin, to Cyprus, while Paul went with Silas on a second journey to Asia Minor. Barnabas is sometimes referred to by Paul in his letters – always with great respect.

Barnabas was another background figure and yet the kind of person on whom the more well-known Paul needed to depend. Think of other examples of such personalities in the Bible, in history and in contemporary life.

Imagine that Barnabas is applying for an appointment as minister of a church on a new housing estate and has asked you to act as referees. Divide into groups of two or three, each to write a reference. Then share them with the larger group.
- What are the main challenges which speak to you in your situation?

A girl whose name is not recorded
Read Acts 16.16-40. This story is very similar to Gospel accounts of Jesus exorcizing demon-possessed people. In each case the demons recognized Jesus. 'I know who you are ... Jesus the Son of God' (see Mark 1.24; 5.6-7). What significance do you think the Gospel writers attached to these cries?

Notice how the casting out of the spirit of Python from the girl in Acts 16 actually advanced the gospel.
- Reflect together on the significance of this.
- What challenges come from the exorcism?

Notice how the girl had been exploited by her masters. Together make a list of ways in which children and young people are exploited worldwide today.
- How can ordinary people like ourselves challenge these evils?

How can ordinary people like ourselves challenge these evils?

We are called
1. Read again the words of Albert Schweitzer on page 29, and reflect on them.
2. Share with one another how you see each other's roles in the church and community. How far do these roles complement one another?
3. Spend some time in quiet, reflecting individually on what you perceive to be your calling.

PRAYER
Pray for one another in the roles you have named. Then, in ever-increasing circles, pray for others who serve in difficult and challenging situations in your church, your community, and other parts of the world.

ACTION
Identify someone in your group, or in your church, who is seeking to fulfil a difficult role. Decide what you can do together to support him or her.

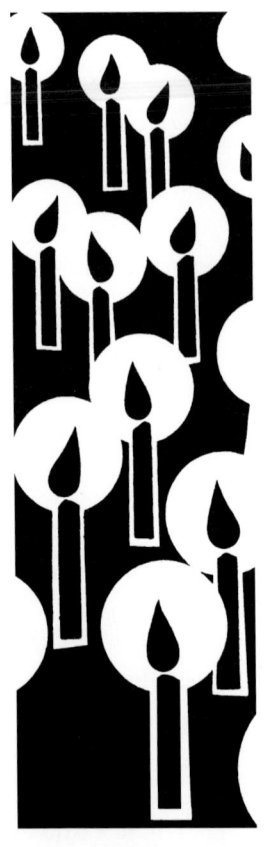

NOTES
BY
DONALD HILTON

CALLED TO LEAD

Study 1 *Patterns of leadership*

AIM
To consider different styles of leadership and seek to identify those most appropriate to Christian leadership.

Keynote passages
Exodus 3.1-15
Exodus 4.10-17
Numbers 11.10-17
Judges 17.1-6
1 Samuel 8.1-22

Preparation
Copy the diagrams below on to a large sheet of paper, or make photocopies of this page.

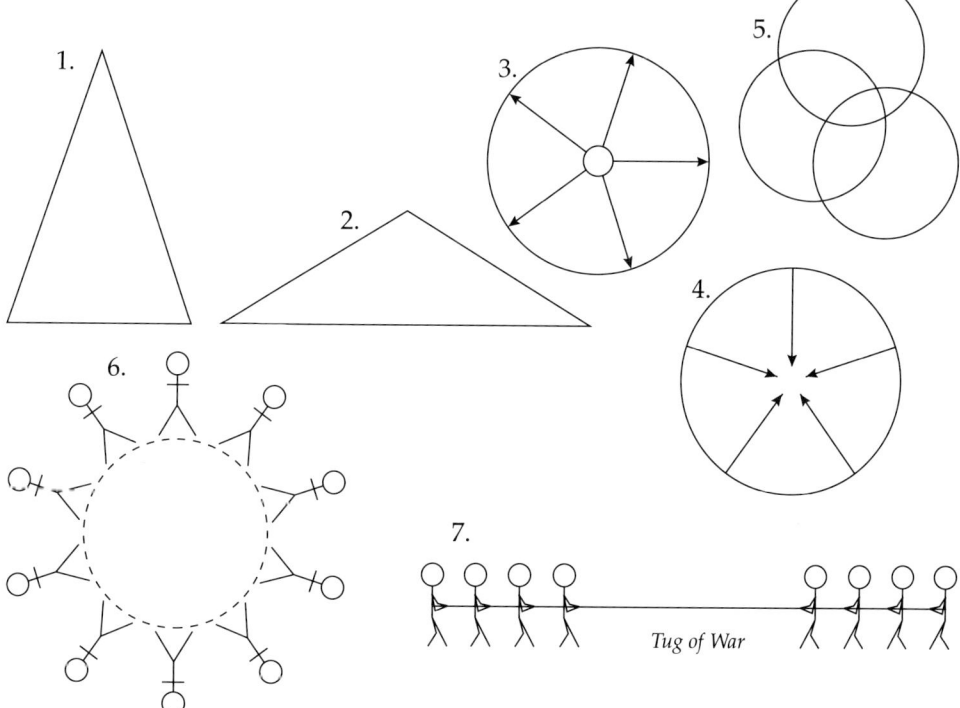

Way in
Ask the group to think about the patterns and pictures above. Each diagram can be seen to describe a different style of leadership. Working individually and in silence,

let them decide what style of leadership the patterns and pictures suggest and which seems most appropriate to Christian leadership.

Discussion: Strengths and weaknesses
No style of leadership is perfect in human hands, and changing situations encourage different forms of leadership, so members of the group may not have chosen the same pattern. Compare their choices and why they made them. Consider the chosen pattern(s) in the light of the following comments:

> 'I have never been a man of ready speech, never in my life, not even now that thou hast spoken to me.'
> *Exodus 4.10*

> '(The seventy elders) will share with you the burden of taking care for the people; then you will not have to bear it alone.'
> *Numbers 11.17b*

> 'In those days there was no king in Israel and every man did what was right in his own eyes.'
> *Judges 17.6*

> 'They have not rejected you (Samuel), it is I (God) whom they have rejected.'
> *1 Samuel 8. 7-8*

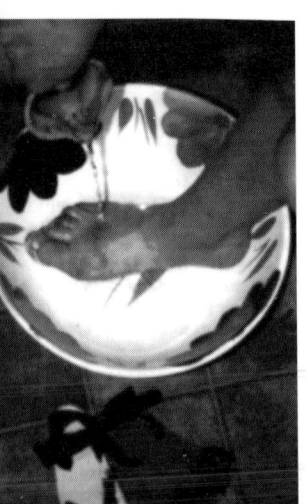

Photo from L'Arche Community

Effective leadership
Invite the group to spend a few moments in silence, remembering people who have been effective leaders in their own experience. Then ask them to summarize in one sentence the nature of their leadership and why it had such an influence on them.

Releasing gifts; discovering leadership
A local church in a deprived urban area of Britain organized an arts centre in which professional artists helped local residents to discover latent skills in painting, pottery, glass-work, carpentry, carving etc. An Arts Festival was planned to display the work achieved. One contributor who had always seen herself as 'one of this world's losers' discovered painting skills she never knew she had. One of her paintings was independently valued at £50. The money was fine, but better was the fact that her gifts were valued for the first time in her life. From such an affirmation of skills new leadership can emerge.

From such an affirmation of skills new leadership can emerge

ACTION

In your church, undoubtedly there are skills and abilities of which even the people who possess them are not aware. What event could you plan which might release these gifts, and thus reveal new leadership potential for your church or wider community?

PRAYER

Lord God,
this we have learned in the community of faith,
for this we give you thanks:
Until we hear with each other's ears
your word is indistinct, unclear.
Until we see with each other's eyes
we live in shadowed half light.
Until we walk as pilgrim friends
we stumble and are quick to fall.
Until we love and let love conquer all mistrust and fear
we are pale shadows of the Christ we serve.
Give us ears and eyes and strengthened steps
and make our common search for truth
a gift of love we offer to each other.

For next week
In preparation for next week's study, invite the group to find a poem, paragraph of prose, an item from a newspaper, or to be prepared to tell briefly the story of someone whose commitment to leadership involved suffering. Suggest that, although some well-known people can be mentioned, it would also be valuable to hear of a mother who suffered for her children, a husband who cared for a sick wife etc.

Study 2   *Called to joy? to suffering?*

AIM

To recognize through personal experience and the experience of others that leadership can bring both joy and suffering.

Preparation
You will need a supply of small candles or night-lights and a secure table on which they can be placed when lit.

Keynote passages
1 Kings 3.4-15
Isaiah 52.13 to 53.12
Matthew 4.18-25
Matthew 5.13-16
Mark 10.32-45
1 Timothy 3.1-13
Philippians 2.1-11

Way in
Read Isaiah 52.13 to 53.6 and then play a recording of the aria, 'He was despised' from Handel's *Messiah*.

Reflection – Lights in the world
Invite the group to contribute the items of poetry or prose they have brought telling of people whose committed leadership has caused them to suffer. After each contribution the reader should light a candle or night-light saying:

   'I light this candle for ...

Conclude the series of contributions with this story from Myanmar (formerly known as Burma):

During the Japanese conquest of Burma, British troops were retreating. A small group of Burmese Christians gave the fleeing soldiers shelter and food. Other Burmans informed on them and they were hauled before the military. 'You have been helping the enemy so you must die,' they were told. Pleading for their lives in vain they asked for time to prepare themselves by prayer. As they knelt they were cut to pieces. One girl was just seventeen. After the war a confirmation service was held and the Bishop noticed that one of the people to be confirmed had been a prominent anti-Christian leader. He asked how he had become a Christian. 'It was those girls in the village,' he said. 'I knew they had something I did not have.'

Many other similar stories can be found in anthologies published by the National Christian Education Council.

Discussion: Sorrows and joys
Discuss what it means in the present day to respond to the invitation of Jesus, 'Follow me'. Try to bring out the potential for both joy and sorrow in Christian commitment and Christian leadership. Encourage the group to tell their own stories of discipleship and leadership they have both given and received.

Story: Purpose out of sorrow
In 1996, Philip Lawrence, a head-teacher in a London school, was stabbed to death by a schoolboy. The teacher was trying to calm a potentially serious situation outside the school gates in which a group of teenagers were

attacking a scholar. After the trial of the attacker, the teacher's widow Frances Lawrence, a committed Christian, appealed for a renewal of morality in Britain and, in particular, for the abolition of 'combat knives'. Her leadership potential was quickly recognized and, in a pre-election period, the issues she raised were taken up by the major political parties. (N.B. *This study was written soon after the event and before the effectiveness of the appeal was known*).

Reflect on what effect, if any, Frances Lawrence's campaign has had. If it has been effective, ask why and what it teaches us about leadership on future occasions. If it has faded from memory ask why this has happened and also what the implications are. Think about public response and political action.

If you do not live in Britain, think of a similar situation in your own country and the response it evoked.

Worship

Quietly play the excerpt from Handel's *Messiah* again, reading Philippians 2.1-11 against the background of the music.

ACTION

If you had ideas about the action suggested last week, how will you follow this up?

NOTES BY JANE ASHPLANT

THE POWER OF PRAYER

Study 1 *What is your God like?*

Keynote readings
Genesis 18.20-31
Isaiah 38.1-20
Psalm 85
Luke 3.21-22
Luke 6.12-16
Luke 11.1-13

AIM
To explore the way in which our image of God affects the way we pray.

Preparation
You will need an icon, or picture of Jesus, paper, pencils, a candle and matches.

Way in
Focus on the icon (or picture). Try to describe what you see. How difficult is it to describe God?

In pairs, discuss and write down all the words you can think of which describe God, and then compare your lists.
- Which words most closely describe your personal image of God?

An angry God
Read Psalm 85.
- How many different images of God can you discover?
- Does a consistent picture of God emerge?
- Is this a God who can be trusted?
- Is there anything in our experience which makes this God seem particularly real?
- Does this God inspire devotion?
- How might we approach such a God?

Sheila Cassidy in *Words for Today 1998*, writes:

'I can imagine the people of Bosnia praying this Psalm, just as the Hebrew exiles prayed it thousands of years ago. "Lord, will you be angry with us for ever? When will the fighting stop?" It would be a good prayer in a drought too: "Lord, so long, so long? When will you send us the rain? Our cattle are dying, the earth is parched, our children starve? When, O Lord, when?"

Perhaps this the commonest age-old heresy: that God is a sort of Santa Claus who sends the sun and rain, and makes the land fertile if he's in a good mood, but withholds it if he's cross with us or just plain dyspeptic. But the Christian God isn't like that: he doesn't withhold the rain; he dies of thirst at the withered breast along with the rest of us.

I see an important issue here: we have a human need to pray for help in time of trouble: we cry to God as a child cries out to a parent. But here, I believe, the simile breaks down. We need to pray: but God does not need our prayers. I do not believe in a God who will withhold bread or rain from his people until they pray for it. It's making God into a monster: like a parent who won't give his hungry child a biscuit until he says 'please'. That may be the way we train our children, but I don't believe it's the way God trains us!'

A giving God
'Ask, and it will be given to you; search, and you will find; knock, and the door will be opened for you.'
Luke 11.9 (NRSV)

- Does this promise make it easier or more difficult to approach God in prayer?

'Your Father knows what you need before you ask him.'
Matthew 6.8b (NRSV)

- Do we believe in a God who knows our every need?
- Is it our experience that God meets our needs, or are there times when our prayers seem to be unanswered?
- How does that make us feel?
- Are we more or less likely to ask again?

A loving God
Read Luke 3.21-22.
- How might parents prepare a child to face a difficult challenge?
- How important is it to know that we are loved and accepted?
- Think about the kind of God who affirms us and shows us how much we are loved. How do we relate to this God in our own experience? How might we approach such a God in prayer?

Think about the kind of God who affirms us and shows us how much we are loved

PRAYER

Light the candle and try to focus on thoughts of God. Use the icon if you find it helpful. Concentrate on how you might respond to the ways in which God reveals himself.

God of love and mercy,
you are far beyond our imagination,
but you allow us to catch glimpses of you along the way.
Help us to remain open to your presence,
and make us always willing to be surprised by you.

ACTION/REFLECTION

Try to give more thought to your own images of God. Think about how they affect the way you approach God in prayer – both individually and as a church community.

Study 2   'I have called you by name'

Keynote readings
Luke 18.1-14
Luke 22.39-46
Acts 4.23-31
Acts 12.11-19
Acts 14.21-28
Colossians 1.3-14

AIM

To recognize that God communicates with us in our difference.

Preparation

You will need
– to find a story from a newspaper/magazine about someone to whom your group will be able to relate;
– paper and pencils.

Way in

Read to the group the newspaper/magazine story you found. Discuss what it is that helps or hinders empathy with the other person. How close can you get to imagining yourself in the other person's situation?

Putting yourself 'in another's shoes'

Read the story of Jesus in Gethsemane – Luke 22.39-46. Think about each of the characters in the story:
- How might they have felt?
- What might they have been thinking about?
- What happened up to this point and what was about to happen?
- Do you think any of the characters knew what was going to happen?

Ask each member of the group to imagine s/he is one of the disciples, or Jesus. Make sure that they have all chosen a different character. Ask them to close their eyes while you read aloud the story again. Leave a minute or two for silent reflection, and then ask:
- What did you see and hear?
- How did it feel?

How different we are
Discuss the difficulties in trying to imagine someone else's experience.
- How do those difficulties relate to the positive differences between individual human beings?
- Would we need any imagination if God made us all the same?

God values our uniqueness
Read Isaiah 43.1-4. This passage is about God's promise to restore the nation of Israel. The people are in exile, but they are given the promise of a rich future. God says, 'I have called you by name, you are mine' (NRSV). They are not only restored but also called by name for a specific purpose.
- What do you hear God saying about the future to the community and nation in which you live? How do you see God responding to the prayers of your people?
- Think of the many peoples of the world. Ask members of the group to mention some of them, and after each country, say the words, 'I have called you by name, you are mine.'

We may also understand these words on an individual basis. God says to each of us, 'I have called you – *Martha* – by name, you are mine.' Try inserting your own name into this phrase. Does it help you to feel loved and accepted by God? Do you feel affirmed as a unique individual?

Look up the following texts: Psalm 23; Isaiah 49.16; Jeremiah 31.3; Luke 12.24; 1 Corinthians 6.20.
- How does this sense of being loved and valued by God affect the way we pray and how we see the fruits of our prayer?

Would we need any imagination if God made us all the same?

How does this sense of being loved and valued by God affect the way we pray and how we see the fruits of our prayer?

PRAYER/REFLECTION

Discuss the special characteristics which make each person a unique individual. Mark your own on a piece of paper and write the words *'Thank you God for ...'* next to each of them.

Loving God, you have made us all
and called us by name to follow you.
Thank you that, even though we are so different,
you love us all equally.
Help us always to be honest with you
and true to ourselves. Amen

ACTION

Determine to be confident about yourself as an individual, and as a group, created and called by God. Listen carefully to discern what the specific call of God for you might be.

> *Listen carefully to discern what the specific call of God for you might be*

THE KINGDOM IS FOR CHILDREN

Notes by Rosemary Wass

Study 1 *The Kingdom and the Convention*

AIM
To place our Christian responsibility towards children in the world context.

Keynote readings
Genesis 21.1-20
Genesis 22.1-19
1 Samuel 3.1-20
Luke 2.41-52
John 6.1-13
Mark 9.33-37
1 Timothy 4.6-16

Preparation
If possible, write to The United Nations Committee For Children asking for a copy of The Convention On The Rights Of The Child.

Address of UNICEF: 55 Lincoln's Inn Fields,
London WC2A 3NB
Tel: 0171 405 5592, Fax: 0171 405 2332.

Way in
Begin the session by asking people to think about children known to them. Think about the setting in which they have seen children this week. Encourage them to make a list of what they saw, e.g. running, playing, watching, painting, climbing etc.

Compile a group list, each naming a different activity until the list of ideas is exhausted.

- Would all the activities be understandable across language barriers?
- Would any need any verbal explanation?
- Were they group activities, or solitary activities?

Looking at the world's children
Childhood is a time of hope and promise for many children in the world. For others, it is a time of hardship and poverty when children are forced to become old before their time; some never get beyond their early years.

Children were undervalued by adults in biblical times, and all these years later we know of children who are exploited and abused, unloved and abandoned, children who are denied education, a home and a name.

- Can we list the causes of some of these situations? *(war, refugees, poverty etc.)*

We have a dream ...

Imagine a world where Jesus' values for children prevailed. Look at each of the keynote readings given for this study and create an ideal picture. The basic needs of all children would be met.

The World community has technically made its declaration of commitment to children in *The Convention On The Rights Of The Child*. The Convention has 54 Articles in all, and are about Children's Rights and about how adults and governments should work together for the good of all children ('child' is defined as anyone under 18 years of age).

From a Chinese paper-cut by students at Nanjing Theological Seminary, China

Has your government ratified the Convention?
Ratification means that there is a solemn agreement to obey the law written down in the Convention. Here are some examples of the Articles contained in the Convention:

Article 14: You (a child) have the right to think what you like and be whatever religion you want to be. Your parents should help you learn what is right from wrong.

Article 16: You (a child) have the right to a private life. For instance, you can keep a diary that other people are not allowed to see.

Article 28: You (a child) have a right to education. Primary education must be free and you must go to primary school. You should also be able to go to secondary school.

Discuss these Articles in pairs. Relate them to any of the Bible passages you have explored under this theme.

PRAYER

Think of two or three joys/concerns about children that you have, and form them into a prayer. These prayers may then form the closing prayer as a group before sharing in the saying of the Grace.

Study 2 *Hearing children*

AIM
To recognize the sounds of children and what is required to turn them into laughter.

Keynote readings
Deuteronomy 11.18-21
Colossians 3.18-21
Leviticus 20.1-5
Matthew 2.13-18
Mark 9.42-48
Isaiah 66.7-14
Mark 10.13-16

Way in
Children draw us like magnets: their actions, their appearances, their innocence, their naiveté, their ability to grow, their personality, their expressions, their voices.

In a world gathering, where language may be a barrier, it only takes the cry of a child to unite a room full of people. The voice of a child speaks every language, and every person who hears understands and wants to turn that cry into a chuckle of laughter. Our cultures may give us different ways of doing it, but we all have the same goal.

As the group meets today, encourage them to think again of children they have met during the week. Ask them to think of the sounds those children made and again make a mental list *(sucking, laughing, hiccups, shouting ...)*.

Biblical reflection
In pairs, now reflect on the following passages and imagine the sounds of the children described in them: Matthew 2.13-18; Mark 9.42-48; 10.13-16; Isaiah 66.7-14. Share the sounds with the whole group.

Campaigning for children
A Chilean poet wrote, 'Many things we need can wait, the child cannot ... To him/her we cannot say tomorrow. His/her name is today.'
- What are the urgent things to secure for the good of the world's children?
- What can we do about them?
- Whose co-operation should we seek?

ACTION
Identify something from your discussion that you can do as a group.

PRAYER
Use the following as a concluding prayer, or as a discussion starter.

Litany for children

WE PRAY FOR CHILDREN
who put chocolate fingers everywhere
who like to be tickled
who jump in puddles, oblivious of the consequences
who have no sense of time or routine
whose shoes are always missing at school-time ...

AND WE PRAY FOR THOSE
who stare at photographers as if from another planet
who have never had a pair of new shoes ...
who have never had the chance to be children
who only know a world of abuse

WE PRAY FOR CHILDREN
who give us sticky kisses and fistfuls of dandelions
who hug us in a hurry and forget their dinner money
who sing their hearts out to their own tune ...
who have imaginary friends and conversations

AND WE PRAY FOR THOSE
who don't have a room to call their own
who can't find any bread to steal
who watch their parents watching them die
whose minds are full of violent memories
who don't feel important to anyone else

WE PRAY FOR CHILDREN
who spend their pocket money before it's actually in their pocket
who throw tantrums in the supermarket and pick at their food
who hide possessions under their bed and leave a ring around the bath ...
whose tears we sometimes laugh at and whose smiles can make us cry

AND WE PRAY FOR THOSE
who will eat everything they have chance of
who have never had a medical or visited a dentist
who know nobody to spoil them
who go to bed hungry and cry themselves to sleep
who do not know the meaning of the word security, of being safe

WE PRAY FOR CHILDREN
who long to be hugged and given a name and a family
and for those who fill our lives and make us feel special.

*© Rosemary Wass (First published in MAGNET,
the magazine for the Women's Network of the
Methodist Church, Winter 1994)*

NOTES
BY
EDMUND BANYARD

MAKING SENSE OF LIFE

Study 1   *Proverbs and daily living*

Keynote readings
Proverbs 1.1-9
6.6-11
11.20
15.17
17.19b; 23.1-8
17.16
23.13

AIM
To consider how the Book of Proverbs might help in choices and decisions which have to be made in everyday life.

Way in
Read each of the passages in the margin. You may not wholly agree with some of them, or think them all applicable to the world you know today; yet all raise important issues. Decide together which you consider to be the most worthy of discussion for your group and list them in order of priority. You have now made your agenda for this meeting.

You have made your own list to work from, but here are a few comments you might care to consider on some of the themes which arise from the Bible passages –

Learning from the wisdom of the past
- Are we too inclined to think that in a world of ever-advancing technology we have little to learn from the past? Even from our religious heritage?
- What danger do you see for a society if it no longer acknowledges that it needs to learn from previous generations?

Bringing up children
In recent years there has been a growing awareness of the need to protect children from abuse of one kind or another. The concept of 'Children's Rights' has been widely accepted.
- How does this fit in with proper correction and discipline?
- Is there any conflict here?

Are we too inclined to think that in a world of ever-advancing technology we have little to learn from the past?

Finding role models
There are strong pressures on both the young and those in middle life to 'make something' of themselves. There are warnings here against the Proud, the Rich, the Shady Dealer, the Miser (Proverbs 17.19b; 23.1-8).
- What other role models, good or bad, might you add?
- What role models would you want to recommend?

Eating and drinking
According to the Revised Standard Version (RSV), Proverbs 15.17 advocates vegetarianism. Read it with the preceding verse (16) to get the more general emphasis. The suggestion is that we should eat to live rather than live to eat. What guidelines do you set yourselves in the matter of eating and drinking?

The use of money
- What advice does Proverbs 17.16 give on gambling and lotteries?
- There are plenty of other ways of using money which from the Christian viewpoint might be regarded as foolish or irresponsible. How do you see the use of money? So much for God, and the rest to do with as you like? Or what?

Purposeful living
'Go to the ant thou sluggard' is certainly an attack on apathy and a call to purposeful living. Yet is being industrious a sufficient end in itself? How important is the purpose, the goal?

Right dealing with others
Weights and scales suggest small-scale dealings in the market-place which may not present so much in the way of problems today; but what areas of life present the need for an urgent call to right dealing with others?

PRAYER
Your discussions will almost certainly have thrown up concerns about some aspects of life today. You have shared them with one another. Now share them in prayer with God.

What guidelines do you set yourselves in the matter of eating and drinking?

How do you see the use of money?

Is being industrious a sufficient end in itself?

*When we come to you
and call you Lord,
look for your help
to carry out our plans,
throw everything upon you
except the question,
'Which way would you have us go?'
Forgive us our foolishness
and help us to become
more willing to listen,
more willing to be redirected,
that we may honour you as Lord
in deed as well as word.*

From *Heaven and Charing Cross* (NCEC 1996)

ACTION

Make a note of any issues you have discussed which seem to you to be particularly important and watch out for others as you follow next week's readings.

Study 2   *More Proverbs and daily living*

Keynote readings
Proverbs 5.11-13
18.4-8 & 13
11.13; 26.23-28
23.29-35; 31.4-7
16.31
25.6-7; 21-22
31.10-31

AIM

To continue considering how passages from the Book of Proverbs might help in the choices and decisions which have to be made in everyday life.

Way in

Have a short light-hearted session recalling sayings/proverbs your parents or grandparents might have been fond of quoting. Do you see any basic difference between these and the passages you have been reading? Now, as you did last week, make a list of topics which emerge from the Bible passages given in the margin, and decide together which you consider to be most worthy of discussion. List them in order of priority.

Again here are a few comments you might care to consider on some of the themes which could well be on your list.

Speech and gossip
We are probably very aware of the dangers of uncontrolled tongues, but what of the popular press and radio and television programmes which pry into private lives? When is this justified? When not?

Drug abuse and alcoholism
The problems are well-known. Consider what is lacking in society that so many should want to turn to these artificial and often dangerous stimuli.

The sexual impulse
The writer of Proverbs was quite simply warning of the dangers of promiscuity. Today many see sexual education as starting from the assumption that young people will be promiscuous anyway. What are the group's thoughts on this?

The matriarch
The Book of Proverbs ends with the beautiful poem picturing the perfect wife. Of course it belongs to a different age and a different way of life; but what qualities might we want to emphasize if we were trying to define for our own time the good wife, the good husband?

Old age
There are societies, e.g. in Madagascar, where respect is naturally given to the elderly just because they are elderly. In much of the western world the current fashion is to glorify the young. What particular and valuable contribution do you think the elderly are able to make to society?

From Old to New Testament
Proverbs 25.6-7 is surely what Jesus draws on when he speaks of taking a lower rather than a higher seat when invited to a feast, and verses 21 and 22 form the magnificent climax to Romans 12. Does this encourage us to look any more closely at the wisdom literature?

What qualities might we want to emphasize if we were trying to define for our own time the good wife, the good husband?

What particular and valuable contribution do you think the elderly are able to make to society?

PRAYER

Remember with thanksgiving the wisdom of past ages and pray for the humility and understanding to profit from the experience of past generations.

We come to you our God and Father,
because you are the same
from generation to generation.
Yet when we listen, really listen,
there is always something new,
something startling
in what you are saying to us.
At times we are shaken,
at times we are hurt,
yet we know we must still listen,
and listening, we learn that your Word
is always a living Word,
and that the work to which you call us
is always a contemporary task.

ACTION

Among the issues you have discussed and thought about in the past two weeks are there any which you feel called to follow up in further study or by some positive involvement?

> *The work to which you call us is always a contemporary task*

EXAMINE ME, O GOD

NOTES BY
PHILIP BARKER

Study 1 *Looking in*

AIM
To prepare ourselves to welcome God's intervention in our lives.

Keynote readings
Exodus 32.7-14
Deuteronomy 30.15-20
Isaiah 46.1-9
Isaiah 59.9-15
Psalm 51.1-10
Psalm 139.1-24

Interruptions!
Henri Nouwen in *Beyond the Mirror* claims that interruptions in everyday life 'have most revealed the divine mystery'. This was part of his life.

A developing relationship
Etty Hillesum, a young Jewish woman who died in Auschwitz, wrote in her diaries of 'a deep well' within her, and in it, she said, was God. But she had to struggle with the problem of digging out 'the stones and grit' which often seemed to bury God in her experience. So she had to keep on digging him out again. She saw this difficult process as an integral part of her spirituality.
- Do we share this experience of God being deep inside us?
- What other ways of describing God's close involvement in our lives do we find helpful?

Paul Tillich, in *The Shaking of the Foundations*, says that the modern way of escaping God is to keep actively making plans and carrying them out and to rush ahead 'as quickly as the beams of sunrise', to achieve as much as possible. But, he adds, 'God's hand falls heavily upon us.'
- Identify the 'stones and grit' that can bury God.
- How can we move them so that God can surface once more?

To catch us out, or help us through?
   'I fled Him, down the nights and down the days,
   I fled Him, down the arches of the years;
   I fled Him, down the labyrinthine ways
   Of my own mind; and in the midst of tears
   I hid from Him, and under running laughter ...'
               From The Hound of Heaven, Francis Thompson

Is there any escaping God?

Read Psalm 139, especially verses 7-12 and 23-24.
- Is there any escaping God?
- What is God's motive for watching us? Is it to catch us out, or with some other intention?

The clear message of Psalm 139 is that as we allow God to examine our lives, our relationship with him will grow and deepen, and we shall be strengthened for the good.
- Do we feel that he is just waiting to catch us out as soon as we make a mistake, or is his intention to support and encourage us when things are difficult?
- As we allow him to examine our lives, will relationships grow increasingly uneasy, or will they be strengthened for the good?

PRAYER

God be in my head, and in my understanding;
God be in my eyes, and in my looking;
God be in my mouth, and in my speaking;
God be in my heart, and in my thinking;
God be at mine end, and at my departing. Amen

Book of Hours, London 1514

ACTION

For this week, try to keep a written note of unexpected things that reveal God to you. On the other side of the page, write down daily examples of how you need God's grace.

Study 2 *Looking out*

Keynote readings
Luke 11.37-52
Luke 12.1-3
Luke 13.1-5
Mark 7.1-23
1 Timothy 1.12-17

AIM

To receive God's forgiveness and face up to its effect on our lives.

Comparing notes

Spend time sharing together experiences of the last week that have challenged or deepened your faith. If people are prepared to mention examples of forgiveness and grace being needed in their lives, encourage them to do so *(but the group must respect any wishes to maintain confidentiality).*

God's grace, faith and love

Although sin has to be acknowledged as it affects our relationship with God, once we repent and sincerely seek his forgiveness we can delight in his grace and mercy. It is encouraging to share such experiences, e.g. read 1 Timothy 1.12-14. We must turn our thoughts away from ourselves and focus on God's amazing grace.

Experiencing forgiveness

It is important for us to have the experience of receiving God's forgiveness, and it may be appropriate for people to affirm this together with some suitable words, e.g:

Christ Jesus came into the world to save sinners.
Let us hear the word of grace – OUR SINS ARE FORGIVEN!
Amen. Thanks be to God.

Share examples of receiving forgiveness from another person and talk particularly about the sense of relief and release which it brought.

How things change!

Read Luke 11.42-46.
- Share experiences of receiving God's forgiveness. Was it just a matter of feeling better?
- Were there other consequences?
- Work out how it could affect our attitudes to others both locally and nationally.

Receiving God's forgiveness is not only about feeling better inside; its effect is proved by the actions and attitudes that result. The Gospel readings this week suggest that we cannot revel in God's grace and still be hypocritical or irresponsible, nor can we judge others or make excuses for ourselves. At a personal and community level (and sometimes nationally) we have to take action to put right injustice and demonstrate compassion.

In July 1996, Nelson Mandela visited England and addressed some 10,000 people in Trafalgar Square, London. Speaking from the balcony of South Africa House, he said:

> *We must turn our thoughts away from ourselves and focus on God's amazing grace*

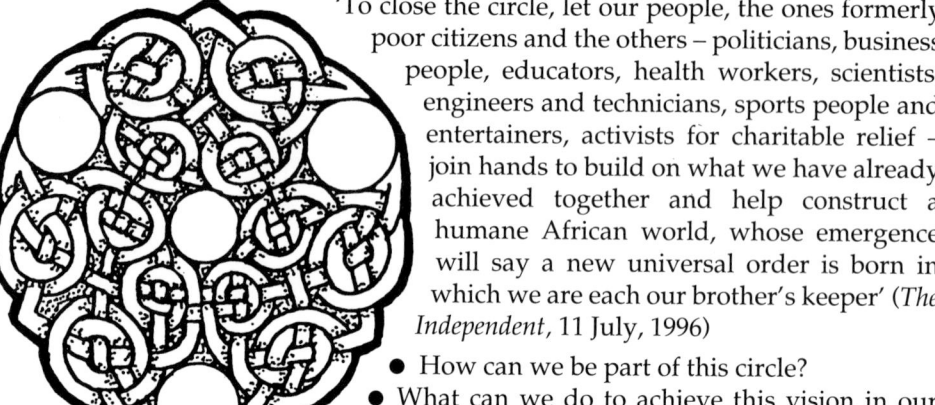

'To close the circle, let our people, the ones formerly poor citizens and the others – politicians, business people, educators, health workers, scientists, engineers and technicians, sports people and entertainers, activists for charitable relief – join hands to build on what we have already achieved together and help construct a humane African world, whose emergence will say a new universal order is born in which we are each our brother's keeper' (*The Independent*, 11 July, 1996)

- How can we be part of this circle?
- What can we do to achieve this vision in our neighbourhood and community?

How can we be part of this circle?

PRAYER

Make the local issues discussed the basis for prayers. Conclude with:

The Kingdom of God is justice, peace and joy.
May they be established on earth and let them begin with us. Amen

ACTION

As a group, decide on some definite actions resulting from your discussion. Aim to make time for progress reports – next week and in a month's time.

BLESSED ARE THE POOR?

NOTES BY
MAGALI DO NASCIMENTO CUNHA

Study 1 *God's preference for the poor*

AIM

To reflect on the meaning of God's preference for the poor.

Keynote readings
Amos 8.4-7
Amos 6.1a, 4-7
Deuteronomy 15.1-11
Leviticus 19.1-4, 9-10
Psalm 113
Luke 1.46-55

Sharing our own stories

For about 15 minutes, in pairs share with one another what kind of contact you have had with poverty. Are you poor? Have you ever been poor? Do you have contact with poor people? How do you (or did you) feel, about this experience? Uncomfortable? Open? Share with the whole group some of your reflections.

Sharing stories from Brazil

Read to the group the following story:

Doña Ester is 65 years old. Like almost everybody who lives in the Baixada Fluminense, an area on the outskirts of Rio de Janeiro City, her family came from the countryside for a better life in the city. Now she is a widow and the pension she receives from the government is very small. She has to work to support her family. She is a housemaid for a family in a wealthy area in Rio. They pay her the minimum salary to clean the house, to cook, and to iron clothes. Every day she has to wake up at 4 a.m., clean her house and cook before going to work. It takes her two hours to get there and at 8 p.m. she comes home to finish her housework. She never sleeps before 11 p.m. This is the normal life for many Brazilian women. But she says the best thing in her life is to go to church. She is a member of an organized group of women and of a group that visits families in need to show love and solidarity. God deserves our praise because God cares. People like Doña Ester can be forgotten by people of this world but God is ready to give them strength and dignity.

After reading the story, allow two minutes for individual reflection on the following questions:

- Put yourself in the place of Doña Ester. How do you feel being an elderly widow who has to work to increase her income but joins a church group that helps people in need?
- List some differences between the life of a widow in your country and the life of Doña Ester.
- What kind of thing in the life of Doña Ester justifies God's blessing to the poor?

Share your thoughts with the whole group.

Biblical reflection

Together, read aloud Luke 1.46-55, if possible in the same version. Try to discover together what are the links between this passage and the reflections already made.

ACTION

- Invite someone in your area who works, or has worked, alongside poor people to share the experience and how much the poor served as an example for life.
- List what you can do as a group to support this work in your area.

PRAYER

Experience a community prayer: each person in the group says a short spontaneous prayer (just a sentence) and then the whole group concludes by saying together the Lord's Prayer.

Study 2 *Steps to the blessing*

Keynote readings
Luke 16.1-31
Luke 12.13-34
1 Timothy 6.6-19
2 Corinthians 8.1-15

AIM

To reaffirm
- the value of the poor in the Kingdom of God and the rejection of ideologies and messages that deny Jesus' proposal;
- solidarity as an attitude to be recovered at the end of the 20th century.

Sharing our own stories

For 20 minutes, in groups of three people, share personal reflections on the following questions:

- Think of the radical nature of Jesus' proposal and how difficult it is to be a Christian.
- Do you think that it is impossible to accept the challenge of being a Christian as Jesus called us to be?
- Think about your life and try to discover what you have to continue to do, what you have to abandon and what you need to change in order to follow Jesus.

Sharing stories from Brazil

Read to the others the following story:

'Christian is trying to find a space in the queue in that large avenue to avoid stopping at the traffic-lights, but he isn't lucky. Just as he reaches the crossing, green changes to red and a policeman looks at him, intending to give him a fine. Christian stops and grouches. Today everything seems wrong. In the office – only problems. Now he's late to the church meeting, the traffic is like a hell and the traffic-lights seem to persecute him.

His consolation is the meeting in which he's taking part. As soon as he gets there, he knows he'll forget his personal problems and, as magic, he will feel relieved. It is as if he is entering a world of gods. Friends, prayer, conversation on spiritual issues, and that mysterious and involving atmosphere of the church. All these things make him think that this suffering in the traffic is worthwhile.

This vision of the meeting makes him smile. His body relaxes and he feels himself in the hall of this spiritual world. But suddenly, as if coming from nothing, a little ragged boy appears in front of him with a windscreen cleaner in the hands. 'Cleaner' is a way of speaking, because the boy's manners makes the small object look "dirtier". Christian instinctively closes the windows and, using a finger, says "No!". The boy, stubborn as all street boys, approaches and suggests an action towards the windscreen. Christian repeats the "No!" with a firm and decisive voice. The boy approaches more and insists with a sad and tired aspect: "Sir, give me some change, for God's sake! I'm hungry, Sir ..." A feeling of powerlessness invades Christian and he feels paralysed. It seems that time has stopped. He would like to say that he's not got any change, but his voice doesn't come. He feels guilty –

> *Think of the radical nature of Jesus' proposal and how difficult it is to be a Christian*

what of, he doesn't know. He would like to give some change, but his body does not obey him. It seems an eternity comes in this short moment. When this bad feeling is intolerable, the traffic light turns green and car horns rescue him from that 'eternal time'. He feels saved by the madness of the traffic, and leaves the boy. He is back to the rush and his expectation to get to his church meeting on time.'

Extracted and translated from: Se Deus existe, porque há pobreza? A fé cristã e os excluídos (If God exists, why is there poverty? Christian Faith and the excluded) by Jung Mo Sung (Paulinas, 1995).

After reading the story, allow two minutes for individual reflection on the following questions:
- Have you already had an experience similar to the one faced by Christian in the story above?
- Imagine that Christian left the boy at the traffic lights but that image did not leave his mind. That 'bad feeling' continued. How do you explain the bad feeling?
- Use your creativity and continue the story of Christian. Imagine what happened to him on the way to the church, during the service, and afterwards.

Share your thoughts with the whole group.

Reflection

Today some ideologies and theologies deny Jesus' promise and challenge that the poor have the Kingdom and are an example for all who are called Christians. The 'neo-liberal system' praises the market, offers salvation through consumerism and declares the poor guilty of being poor and an obstacle to the total development of the nations. The 'theology of prosperity' preaches that the poor are sinners who are distant from God. If they do what is right and serve the Lord, problems will be solved and financial prosperity will come.

It is time, more than ever, to reaffirm that the Kingdom of God is based on true love, justice, peace, sharing, solidarity, generosity, fellowship, and loyalty to the Lord who was born in a cattle shed, and had no place to lay his head.

There is no need for those who have money and properties to lose them to serve God. There is no need to

*Drawing by Cerezo Barredo.
From El Tayacan, Nicaragua Libre*

It is only necessary to love, have mercy, share, be generous, be available, and to serve without self-interest

be ragged, or resort to begging in the streets, to follow in the steps of the Kingdom. It is only necessary to love, have mercy, share, be generous, be available, and to serve without self-interest. It is time to reaffirm this and renew our covenant with the Lord.

ACTION

Read Luke 6.20-22. Then write a statement, together, denouncing the way people have been taught to become more and more individualistic. Share the word of hope which comes from Jesus in the passage you have just read. Share the statement with as many people as you can. If possible, send it to a newspaper.

PRAYER

Say together:
Dear Lord, here we are, weak, human, full of failures and sin.
We would like to offer you our lives, as they are,
and say again that we believe in you.
We believe in your promise and accept the challenge of following you.
We acknowledge how difficult it is to serve you,
and rely on your help to show us the way.
Have mercy on the poor and the sufferers of our world, O God.
Give us the strength and courage we need to stay alongside them
and overcome all our prejudices and barriers.
Thank you for being our Lord and looking after us as your children.
In Jesus' loving name. Amen

IBRA INTERNATIONAL APPEAL

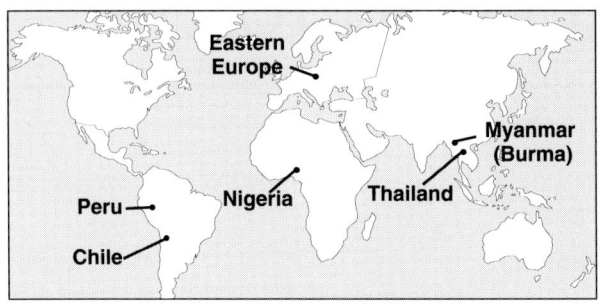

In five continents you will find Christians using IBRA material

Some Christians will be using books and Bible reading cards translated into their local language whilst others use English books. Some of the books are printed in this country but more and more of the books and cards are printed in their own countries. This is done by the IBRA International Fund working through churches and Christian groups and Christian Publishing houses overseas.

Each year we receive more requests for help from the IBRA International Fund, with greater emphasis on helping our overseas friends to produce their own version of IBRA material.

**THE ONLY MONEY WE HAVE TO SEND
IS THE MONEY YOU GIVE,
SO PLEASE HELP US AGAIN BY GIVING GENEROUSLY**

Place your gift in the envelope provided and give it to your IBRA representative, or send it direct to:

The IBRA International Appeal
1020 Bristol Road, Selly Oak
Birmingham Great Britain B29 6LB
Thank you for your help.

Notes by
Keith Johnson

HUMAN RIGHTS

Keynote readings:
Jeremiah 37.11-21
Lamentations 1.1-6
Habakkuk 1.1-4; 2.1-4
Luke 4.16-21
Acts 25.6-12
2 Timothy 1.1-14
Revelation 1.9-20

AIM
To increase our awareness of the worldwide lack of basic human rights and to explore together what we can do to change this.

Preparation
Ask your group to look in their daily newspapers and magazines and cut out and bring any articles or reports of situations in the world behind which there is a grave abuse of human rights.

Way in
From newspaper and magazine articles, share together situations of human rights abuses which are currently in the news.

Biblical reflection
Today we shall focus particularly on prisoners of conscience. Read Jeremiah 37.11-21 and Revelation 1.9-20. Reflect together on the similarities and differences between the biblical accounts and situations currently in the news.

What would you describe as fundamental human rights?

- What would you describe as fundamental human rights?
- Some people argue that human rights are highlighted more than necessary, that we should devote more time and energy to humanitarian service. What do you think?
- It is hard for those of us who live in a relatively free, open society to see and recognize human rights issues (which are often matters of life and death). How far should we concentrate our thoughts, prayers and actions on problems in our own country, and how much should Christians become involved in world issues?

In pairs, read Habakkuk 1.1-4 and 2.1-4. We too live in a violent society. Many more people can be destroyed by one weapon. What do the Churches say to the arms industry?

Over the centuries, the Church has not only overlooked mass violence in wartime; it has supported and encouraged violence between nations, and engaged in it in Christ's name. Think of examples.

Read together Luke 4.16-21. Jesus does not talk about 'Human rights' as such, but what clues does he give us in this passage?
- What other stories, parables and sayings in the Gospels reflect Jesus' deep concern for human rights? Make a list of them.
- How should Christians respond?

Amnesty International

In 1996, a local Amnesty group was given the name of a Vietnamese 'prisoner of conscience' and asked to work for his release. His 'crime' was to oppose his government, albeit peacefully, and join the opposition. Having already been imprisoned for about 16 years, he was then (at the age of 75 and in poor health) given an eleven-year sentence. The Amnesty group has a vague idea where he is imprisoned, but not a precise address, so cannot communicate with him. It is therefore reduced to writing frequently to names on the long list of Vietnamese officials, pleading for his release: the only good feature in all this is that the group will have enough time to mount a solid campaign for the prisoner locally.

PRAYER

Pray for the countries to which you have referred in your discussion, using your Church's Prayer Handbook, and remembering
- people in those countries who are suffering for their beliefs and views;
- those who are tortured and kept in solitary confinement;
- the families of victims of oppression.

ACTION

As an individual, join Amnesty International and help its work – chiefly letter-writing (in the UK, there are well over 100,000 members). Find out if there is a local Amnesty group which you could join, or to which you might be affiliated (there are about 300 such groups in the UK).

There are Amnesty International Sections in most countries of the world. If you cannot find out the headquarters of the section in your country, or do not know if there is one, the International Secretariat (1 Easton Street, London WC1X 8DJ, UK) can help you.

NEW

MORE LIVING PRAYERS FOR TODAY

Compiled by Maureen Edwards

This companion volume to *Living Prayers for Today*, focuses on the Christian festivals and includes some prayers for everyday use. The collection reflects the rich variety of insights so characteristic of IBRA's annual publications. It expresses a strong sense of God's love for the world and each person in it. Through many of the prayers, God, ever-present, suffering and celebrating with all peoples, challenges us to translate our concern into action.

> 'A prayer from Sri Lanka speaks of water falling on dry tea-leaves and bringing out their flavour – many of the prayers in this book did that for me!'
> *Revd Dr Kathleen Richardson OBE,*
> *Moderator, Free Church Federal Council*

UK price £11.99

Order through your IBRA representative or from the appropriate address on page 128.

GOD'S SHALOM

Notes by
Helen Richmond
(Study 1)
and
John R Pritchard
(Studies 2 & 3)

Study 1 *Shalom – healing minds and bodies*

AIM
To share stories of God's healing power in our lives and reflect on our vision of *shalom*.

Keynote readings
2 Kings 5.1-3, 7-15
Luke 7.36-50
John 5.1-18
Colossians 3.12-17
Romans 12.14-20

Helpful resources
Duchrow, U & Liedke, G, *Shalom: Biblical Perspectives on Creation, Justice and Peace* (World Council of Churches)

Ched Myers, *Who will Roll Away the Stone? Discipleship Queries for First World Christians* (Orbis Books, Maryknoll, USA 1994)

Introductory exercise
In pairs tell a story (either from your own life or someone you have been involved with) of pain and brokenness being transformed into wholeness.

Discussion
What makes healing possible?

Taking mission seriously
Read Luke 7.36-50 and John 5.1-18.

Jesus ministered to the broken-hearted, setting the captives free, making the lame walk, offering forgiveness to the sinner. He restored relationships, turned lives around, changed attitudes, made the sorrowful sing for joy. He challenged the views of the powerful and questioned social and religious practices that kept people in bondage.

Part of what it means to be a church that takes mission seriously is to live by a vision of *shalom* – healed bodies and minds, a world where all are included and treated as human beings made in God's image. We may not all describe it in exactly the same way, but those whose lives have been transformed by their encounter with the living

What makes healing possible?

103

Christ, and who identify themselves as belonging to Christ's family, share a vision of wholeness of life as God intends it for all God's children. It is a vision based on God's commitment to this world and love for each person seen most clearly in Christ Jesus.

Quiet reflection
- In what ways have you heard Jesus say to you, 'Take up your mat and walk'?
- What opposition or hurdles have you had to overcome to take up his invitation?

Share your reflections with the group.

New beginnings
Commitment to a vision of *shalom* means living in hope that God's reconciling work can be experienced in our lives. This does not mean that we deny the reality of our own brokenness, or say that the mistakes of the past don't matter. But by facing the pain, naming it, and asking God to deal with it, new beginnings become possible.

Read Colossians 3.12-17 and Romans 12.14-20.

Paul's words about 'forbearing one another' and 'doing good to those who have wronged you' appear to go against everything we are taught to live by.
- How do you understand these strange words?
- How does the willingness to let go of enmity and hatred open up the possibility of healing?
- In what ways does the forbearing of one another also mean that we take each other seriously enough to disagree passionately at times? See Luke 12.51-53.
- Summarize key ways in which the readings this week have helped you to share God's dream of *Shalom* as a healing of bodies and minds.

Begin to imagine!
Contemplate the ways things could be different, and believe that change is possible.
- What small but meaningful steps are you taking to work for change?

What small but meaningful steps are you taking to work for change?

PRAYER *(based on Matthew 25.1-13)*

Lord, how long must we wait?
You seem to be taking your time in coming.
How can we keep our faith alive?
How can we sustain our hope?
How can we keep our lamps burning?
How can we keep our lamps from going out?

We hear Your words whispering to us.
   Keep the dream alive
   Watch and wait
   One day I will return
   One day justice will flow like a river

Help us to believe that despite appearances
You are slowly and surely building your Kingdom.
Help us to keep the dream alive,
help us to wait.

Not passively
but actively.
Not distractedly
but with eyes focused on you
and the new creation you are bringing to birth.

While waiting for Jesus
do not let us become content with the way things are.
Make us impatient
with all that diminishes your image in each other.
While watching and waiting for your Kingdom
keep our lamps burning bright.

                                Helen Richmond
(First published in the Mission Prayer Handbook of the Uniting Church of Australia 1996)

ACTION

No situation was beyond Jesus' ability to transform. In what situations do you find yourself where it would be easier to remain silent, but where you believe God is calling you to raise your voice with conviction, to name truth and expose falsehood or offer words of comfort and support? Decide what you will do about it.

> *Do not let us become content with the way things are*

Study 2 Shalom – healing communities

Keynote readings
Luke 9.51-56
Luke 17.11-19
Acts 8.4-25
John 20.19-23

AIM
To identify areas of brokenness within our immediate community and in wider society and consider what to do about them. *(Note the double meaning of this week's theme: the healing of communities/communities that heal).*

Preparation
Provide a small piece of plasticine for each member of the group (it will need to be warm!)

To start the meeting
Break into the conversation (or break the silence) and ask people to remember a breakage at home. Share how they felt about it – indifferent or upset? – depending what was broken, its value, its associations ...

Ask each person to make a model of anything they like with the plasticine *(allow 3 or 4 minutes)* and say a prayer of thanks to God for sharing with us the gift of creativity.

Then flatten the models. How does it feel? Who has spent hours on a jigsaw, a model, a picture, a meal, only for it to be somehow ruined? *(If the experience is still painful, take time to comfort and support one another).*

Quiet reflection
Think about the broken bits of God's world. Imagine how God feels ...

Bible study
Read together Luke 9.51-56. Share what you know about the people of Samaria.

Recall Jesus' story of the 'Good Samaritan' or invent a version arising from your context.
- Where are the 'fault-lines' (a geological term, to which no blame is attached) in your community, your neighbourhood, your society?
- For whom might you appear as an unwelcoming Samaritan? Who might want to curse (call down fire on) you?
- How can you go about changing the image they have of you?

Who might want to curse you?

Remember that when Jesus spoke of Samaritans, or any foreigners, in a favourable light, he was not popular. Look at Luke 4.25-28. What made the people want to lynch him?

Further discussion

1. Some of the fault-lines you have identified arise because (in the words of a hymn) 'colour, scorn or wealth divide'. Which?
2. Some derive from disagreement on ethical issues, such as abortion, warfare, gay and lesbian relationships.
3. Some are the consequence of different faith-commitments.
   - Do the several types of division require tackling in different ways?
   - Think about the chances of misunderstanding and unpopularity for those who try to mend the fault-lines.
   - How can you support one another in your efforts to be a healing community?

PRAYER

Creator God, author of peace and lover of concord,
fill us with the desire to mend the broken bits of our community,
show us where to begin
and give us the persistence that is both fearless and tireless as we pursue Shalom.

ACTION

1. Read together the following story:

A Scottish hospital chaplain came across a woman who did not recognize him. She was rocking backwards and forwards and was very restless. He indicated to the charge nurse that he thought the visit a waste of time. The nurse challenged him just to hold her hand and time himself for ten minutes (the nurses no longer had time to do that). The chaplain held out his hand and she held it. He spoke quite softly about things that had been going on in the church – the well-attended Saturday coffee morning where there had been a stall of fresh home-baked goods; the lovely Sunday service with the lighting of the Advent candle; the Boys' Brigade parade service. She talked while her hand

How can you support one another in your efforts to be a healing community?

were being stroked, and it did soothe her. The unconnected words did not make sense, and the last five minutes were just silence. The charge nurse let the chaplain out and said, 'She'll be different tonight because you have given her time.'

Decide on 10 minutes' worth of action this week that can build *Shalom*.

2. Contact members of other faith communities locally and discover whether in their scriptures there are stories or teachings about brokenness and healing. How do they react to the idea of a 'Good Samaritan'?

(In the unlikely event that there are no other faith communities in your area, get a friend elsewhere to ask for you).

Decide in the group who will contact whom.

Study 3   *Shalom – healing nations*

Keynote readings
Leviticus 26.6-10
Joel 2.23-32
Sirach 35.12-17
Revelation 22.1-5

AIM
To examine the root causes of unrest and war, reflect on the things that make for peace, and choose a practical way of working for a peace-full world.

Before the meeting
Ask everyone to come with a stone or two from the garden (say 3"-4" in diameter) to build a 'peace cairn'. If most members of the group live in flats or a residential home, pieces of soap could be used instead of stones. Ask each person to think of a specific situation of war or unrest in the news.

'Happy are those who work for peace' (Matthew 5.9)
Bert Bissell OBE, is known for two things. At Vicar Street Methodist Church in Dudley, he led a Bible class which influenced the lives of hundreds of young people over many years. And he built peace-cairns at the summit of various mountains, including Ben Nevis in Scotland, which he climbed regularly (until in his nineties) to witness for peace.

A mini-cairn
Each member in turn places a stone in the middle of the room (floor or table) and says something – or reads a newspaper-cutting – about a particular situation of unrest.

If the group is small you could go round twice. Some situations will be picked up more than once, but you may have five or six to think about.

Getting to the bottom of it
- What do you know about the causes of these conflicts?
- What factors are specific to particular situations?
- What factors are common to several, or all of them?
- What needs to happen to 'give peace a chance'?

Bible study – Joel 2.23-27 – Things that make for peace
- **Water**: indispensable all year round (note the triple reference to rain in verse 23).
- **Enough to be satisfied** (verse 26): 'how much is enough?' Remember the adage about 'enough for everyone's need but not for anyone's greed'.
- **Dignity**: note the twice-repeated 'My people will never be despised again.'

What needs to happen to 'give peace a chance'?

Choose one of the following to discuss, either as a whole group or two smaller groups:

1. In your nation, which of these three elements are present in healthy proportions?
   If they are not, who is suffering?
   What can be done for their healing?
2. Look at each of Joel's emphases in turn: are they pertinent to any of the conflicts you have identified?
   To 'give peace a chance', what must be done in terms of
   (a) physical, material changes and
   (b) changes of attitude?

ACTION
Review your own attitude to
- the weather: Do I complain too easily?
- material things: How much do I need? How can my surplus be useful?
- others: Who do I despise? Why? What does the Lord require of me?

PRAYER

Remember: 'The Lord is a judge who listens ... who does not ignore the orphan, the widow, the humble ...' (Sirach 35.13-14).

Say together
For the healing of the nations,
   Lord, we pray with one accord;
For a just and equal sharing
   Of the things that earth affords.
To a life of love in action
   Help us rise and pledge our word.

All stand; each picks up a stone from the cairn; continue together:
All that kills abundant living,
   Let it from the earth be banned;
Pride of status, race, or schooling,
   Dogmas that obscure your plan.
In our common quest for justice
   May we hallow life's brief span.

                    Fred Kaan © 1968 Stainer and Bell Ltd.

'To a life of love in action Help us rise and pledge our word'

ONENESS IN CHRIST

NOTES BY PENNY FOWLER

Study 1 *Everything in unity with Christ*

AIM
To explore our ideas of 'unity'.

Keynote readings
Ephesians 2.11-19
Ephesians 3.1-21

Preparation
Ask each member of your group, if possible, to draw or bring along a picture that represents her/himself.

What is unity?
Read each of the following three stories to the group *(or ask three of the group to read them)*:

* A small group of musicians plays together. They do not have a conductor to lead them, but one of the violinists leads the group in their playing. They all watch her and so the result is harmony and a sense of working together.

* A church member found it difficult, after the death of her son, to visit the other members of her group for whom she was responsible. As she called at each house she discovered that many of the group had suffered a similar bereavement; support was offered and accepted.

* In his autobiography, Nelson Mandela writes of the time of the arrest and imprisonment of most of the ANC leadership. Many had previously been 'banned persons', which meant that they were not legally allowed to speak with, meet or contact each other. Now the authorities had gathered them all together under one (prison) roof and they were able to share ideas and experiences. Singing, organized activities and a traditional Zulu war dance all caused deep emotions in the hearts of the prisoners. A common history, love of culture and of their country all contributed to the feeling of being linked together.

● What can we learn about unity from these stories?

A common history, love of culture and of their country all contributed to the feeling of being linked together

111

Background to the letter to the Ephesians

In the first century AD the theme of unity was important in people's minds. Stoic philosophers saw order and design in the universe giving it an underlying unity. Large areas of the Mediterranean world had been brought together into the Roman empire, helped by improved communications. The 'mystery' religions fostered a search for unity in the fragmented lives of individuals.

The writer of the letter to the Ephesians contributed to this search for unity, which is a strong theme in the book. This week's readings point to different images of unity, and reasons for it.

Read Ephesians 2.11-19; 3.1-21.
- What are the images of unity portrayed?
- What do these verses teach us about our lives as Christians – as individuals, as members of the Church?

Signs and symbols

1. Various organizations have an emblem that has become associated with the group, such as those drawn below. If the rest of the group do not have copies of this book, pass yours around for everyone to see. What do you think is the significance of each?
   1. *the World Council of Churches' ship;*
   2. *the globe used by Oxfam, an international relief and development organization;*
   3. *the lotus, cross and circle of the Church of South India.*

The emblem of the Church of South India

'The emblem signals the CSI's vision and commitment to fulfil the high priestly prayer of Jesus in John 17.21. These words encircle the Cross and a burning bush, symbolizing a suffering and oppressed people who are assured of hope of liberation. The bush is not the wild thorny plant on the rugged Mount Sinai, but a lotus, in full bloom, opened up in all its radiance, beauty and splendour, burning and yet not consumed. The lotus, in the religious heritage of India, is the symbol of purity. It grows in muddy waters and yet is not stained or contaminated by them, like the disciples of Christ who are in the world and yet not of the world (John 17.11,14,16). The circle, an Indian religious symbol of completeness and righteousness, represents the fullness of life Jesus brings for all. The lotus has one further significance – God is often depicted standing on a fully open lotus flower. As the Church obeys the call of Jesus Christ to unity, it becomes the bearer of hope and life for the whole creation.'

Victor Premasagar – from Words for Today (IBRA, 1997)

2. Look at the pictures or drawings which members of the group have brought, or just simply ask them to write their name.

3. Make an emblem to represent your group by using all these and use it as a poster in worship in your local church, or on some other occasion.

PRAYERS

Using the emblem as a prayer focus, think about the individuals in your group. Ask each member to suggest a subject for prayers – concerns for the individual, for the local and wider area, for needs of the world that have come to your notice recently. Link hands and say the Grace together. Choose a song that celebrates your togetherness.

ACTION

'As God has called you, live up to your calling.'

How will you respond to this – as individuals, as a group, as a church?

Study 2 Gifts to equip God's people

Keynote readings
Ephesians 4.1-16
Ephesians 6.10-18

AIM
To recognize and affirm each others' gifts.

Introductions
In pairs, take turns to talk to each other for five to ten minutes each. Discover something new about your partner, and then introduce him/her to the group.

Read Ephesians 4.11-12 and 1 Corinthians 12.28, and make a list of the gifts mentioned in these two passages.
- Why were the gifts given?
- Think of people in other parts of the Bible.
- What gifts were they given?
- Why were these gifts given?

Ask each member of the group to think of one person who has played an important part in her/his life, and to spend a short time thinking of him/her. Then share your thoughts together – Why were these people important to you? What gifts did they have? How did they use those gifts?

Affirming each other
Give everyone in the group a piece of paper on which they are to write their name at the bottom of the page. They will then pass the paper to the person on their left, who will write at the top of the page what they appreciate about the person who is named. Fold over the top so that the writing is covered and pass it to the next person on the left and so continue the process around the room. Each person will eventually receive the original paper back with six to ten positive expressions of appreciation.

Gifts in society and gifts for the church
Read Ephesians 6.10-18.

Spend a short time thinking about the place where you live.

'Each of us has been given a special gift' (4.7).
'Put on the whole armour provided by God' (6.11).
- What special gifts are needed in your situation?
- What 'weapons' will you need to fight the evil in your community?

What 'weapons' will you need to fight the evil in your community?

PRAYER

In every generation there have been women and men who have been given special gifts – we give thanks for them.

In our generation there are women and men who have been given gifts – help us to recognize and appreciate the gifts of others and in so doing learn to play our part in the building up of the body of Christ.

ACTION

How will you put on and use God's armour?

> *How will you put on and use God's armour?*

NOTES
BY
JOY MEAD

CHRIST COMES IN THE FLESH

Study 1 *The last word*

Keynote readings
1 John 1.1-4
1 John 2.3-11

AIM
To reflect upon how all things may be seen afresh in the light of the coming and teaching of Jesus.

Preparation
You might like to have a bowl of fruit, strawberries if available, as a focal point. It would also be useful to have available examples of rule books for organizations or games. Members of the group might be able to produce examples.

Introducing 1 John
1 John is a bit like an instruction booklet for its time. It was probably written to deal urgently with disturbance within the Christian community and stresses the importance of obeying rules. The author assures us that this will lead to knowledge of God or enlightenment.

How do we know?
- How much can you discover about an organization or a game just by reading the rules? Look at some rule books.
- Read together 1 John 2.3-11.
- Consider these words about baptism from Clement of Alexandria (second century AD): 'It is not the washing alone that makes us free, but also the knowledge: who were we? what have we become? ... what is birth? What is rebirth? (quoted in Kenneth Grayston's *Commentary on The Johannine Epistles* – Epworth). What do you understand by knowledge in this context?
- Look carefully at the way John uses words. Now talk about the 'commands' and the way old rules are being made new.

Read this poem by Kathy Galloway:

Sacrament

In the train,
a beautiful young man in a green jersey,
dark-haired, white-skinned, red-lipped,
ate glowing scarlet strawberries
with an air of dreamy distraction.
Enraptured, savouring this flesh and fruit,
I am in communion with everyone
(lovers, artists, sticky-mouthed children,
ripe girls, men black with dust and dry of throat,
old ladies with cut-glass dishes,
travellers on hidden lanes)
who has ever delighted
in the graceful
taste of strawberries
and beautiful young men
and the word made flesh.

From Talking to the Bones, Kathy Galloway (SPCK)

Again, look at the words. How are their intentions different from those of 1 John?

Now think about how we come to know anything. Are there ways besides commands, instruction, information? What about sensation, perception, insight, surprise, wonder? Find instances in your own life that bridge the gap between imagination and knowledge, when surprise and wonder have made you say: 'Now I understand; now I know with all my being.'

The poet Samuel Taylor Coleridge, feeling dejected and looking at the beauties of nature in the evening light, wrote:

'... I see them all, so excellently fair!
I see, not feel, how beautiful they are.'

Without a feeling of wonder, do we lose the ability to truly know, to love and to dream?

Towards a conclusion

What did you make of the commands? John is never specific about them. They are deeply embedded in the wonder of creation – 'The last word is always the one made flesh' *(Kathy Galloway)*.

'Amazement is the thing'
Alastair Reid

Keynote readings
1 John 3.11-18
1 John 4.7-21
Gospel of John 4.5-30

PRAYER

We have need of awe and wonder:
    that we may see eternity in a grain of sand;
    that we may see the understanding of all
        in the fall of a sparrow;
    that we may see greatness in two pennies on a plate;
    life in a seed that seems to die;
    trust in a baby's reaching hands;

that we may see how Christ the Lord of all
    smiles from the small.
God of all and every truth
help us to look with open eyes
    to see with open hearts.
                      © Joy Mead

Study 2   *A touching place*

AIM

To look at compassion as a way of life and explore the public living-out of the 'Great Hymn of Love'.

Preparation

You might like to think about following the study with a meal, each member bringing something to share with others. Sharing bread, companionship, should be central.

It would also be useful to have available a cassette player and the tape Love from Below *– songs recorded by the Wild Goose Worship Group (available from your local bookseller, or from Wild Goose Publications, Iona Community, 840 Govan Road, Glasgow G51 3UU).*

Love in community

The teaching about love is the enduring part of John's epistles. Read 1 John 4.7-21, the Great Hymn of Love. This is about flesh and blood action: the theology of a concerned heart. Thought is the beginning, feeling makes the connections.

Think about the Greek words for love: *agape* (platonic love) and *eros* (sensual love). How do we get in touch with our feelings (that's what erotic means). How do we make 'a touching place' for others? *If you have a recording of 'A touching place' (from Wild Goose Publications), play it now.*

Compassion
Read 1 John 3.17.

Think about compassion as love in community. Compassion is active and mutual: it's about sharing suffering.

Read together or act out the story in John's Gospel (John 4.5-30), which tells of a meeting between Jesus and the Samaritan woman at Jacob's Well. This is a moving and poignant story of true meeting, of giving and receiving; of compassion, mutuality and letting go.

In his beautiful book *Promised Lands* (© Harper Collins), Paul Vallely tells a similar story:

'There was a cough behind me. It was Maria. She stood for a moment in the pool of light. Her tattered skirt, which had looked dirty and dingy in the gloom of the undergrowth, now looked brilliantly colourful, and the yellow cocoa pods in the large basket slung from her shoulder glinted like gold in the sunshine. She smiled, for the first time, and produced from behind her a small bundle, wrapped in an old cloth.

"You have come far into the plantation with no food," she said. "It is lunchtime." Swinging the basket down to the ground she squatted on a fallen tree and untied the corners of the cloth. Inside was a ball of sticky yellow-white porridge. "It is farofa, cassava flour mixed with palm oil," she said and began to chat to cover my silence. "There is no meat, I am afraid. Cold beans are bad for the digestion; they bring stomach ache. And meat, I am sorry, but we hardly talk about meat these days. But the farofa is good. Come eat. It is good to share."

I looked at the small mound of food. Embarrassed, I began to mutter that I was not hungry.

"Nonsense," she replied. "It is a long way back to the town. I have food; you have none. It is my duty to share with you." She pulled a lump from the yellowy ball and held it out to me.'

Look at mutuality in these stories. What do you learn about the active nature of compassion? Is it pity, or the celebration of shared feelings?

Towards a conclusion

The commandment revealed in the 'Word made flesh' is to love ... a mutual expression ... the basis of right relationship ... sharing of all things ...

PRAYER

If the hunger of others is not my own,
If the anguish of my neighbour in all its forms touches me not,
If the nakedness of my brother or sister does not torment me,
then I have no reason to go to church and live.
Life is this: to love one's neighbour as oneself;
this is the commandment of God.
Love means deeds, not good wishes.
For this reason I commit myself to working
for the necessities of my brothers and sisters.

Javier Torres, Nicaragua
From Solidarity with the people of Nicaragua (Orbis)

> 'Christ is the one who meets us here'
> Iona Community

PREACHERS' HANDBOOK

- For everyone involved in the preparation of sermons and addresses

- Uses the same passages and themes as *Words for Today* and *Light for our Path*

UK price £4.99

Order through your IBRA representative or from the appropriate address on page 128.

ADVENT

Notes by
Edmund Banyard
(Study 1)
Maureen Edwards
(Studies 2 & 3)

Study 1 *Awake! Christ comes to judge*

AIM
To consider the nature of the judgement to which the New Testament bears testimony, why that judgement is an integral part of the 'good news' and what implications it has for our daily living.

Keynote readings
Isaiah 2.1-5
Matthew 24.36-44
1 Peter 4.7-11
Luke 12.4-8
Romans 13.11-14
Matthew 25.31-46

Way in
Quickly list as many different situations as you can where judgement of one sort or another is involved, e.g. law courts, exams, deciding on quality of merchandise, or whether an antique is genuine, competitive sports, etc.

When might judgement be welcomed?
The idea of judgement can sound frightening, but starting from your list see how many instances you can find where judgement might be welcomed, even eagerly sought: e.g. people who believe that they have been unfairly treated may well seek for someone who will give them 'justice'.

Who might welcome God's judgement?
Starting from this week's Scripture passages, consider who might have been longing for a Day of Judgement to redress wrong? Now go on to think of the modern world: who might figure on today's list?

Why the call to be 'awake'?
- We need to be on guard against accepting standards and attitudes which seem harmless, even normal, but which are opposed to the ways to which we are called by God. Where in modern life do you recognize the attitude expressed in Wisdom 2.6-15?
- We are summoned to be ready for the 'Coming of the Son of Man'. Matthew 24.36-44 is but one of the passages in the New Testament where there is this note of urgency. How do you think we ourselves might experience this 'coming'?

How do you think we ourselves might experience this 'coming'?

Consider here Tolstoy's story, *Where Love Is, God Is:*

Martin the Cobbler looks out with great expectancy, from the basement where he works on to a Russian winter scene for he is sure that on the previous evening he heard the Lord promise to visit him this very day. Time passes. He sees a broken old man clearing snow and calls him in for a hot drink. Later he sees a woman poorly dressed for the cold with a baby in her arms, and calls her in to the warm and finds food for her from his meagre store. Last of all he sees a boy who has tried to steal an apple from an apple-seller; both are brought in and reconciled; but of the visitor he really hopes to see there is no sign. The Lord has not come. Sadly as the day ends he takes up his Bible. Then he hears the voice again and he learns that the Lord came in the person of his visitors and all unwittingly he had given him a royal welcome.

And so, the ultimate test

The familiar story in Matthew 25.31-46 sets out the ultimate test. Consider how Christians should face up to this today, first as individuals and then collectively. E.g. have we got the balance right in our church life between 'keeping the show on the road' and reaching out in loving compassion?

PRAYER

There are three distinct, yet interwoven, prayer themes which arise this week:

1. Thanksgiving that the Almighty is indeed just and righteous and that the loving self-giving which we see in Jesus Christ will ultimately triumph over evil.
2. Confession of our own failures to do even the good we recognize, and prayer for forgiveness and grace to amend our lives.
3. Intercession for some of God's most needy children in the world of today.

ACTION

Advent renews the challenge to us all to seek for ways in which we may increase our sensitivity, our awareness. What steps could you take which might help you more readily to recognize the coming of Christ in 'ordinary' everyday situations?

Study 2 *What will endure?*

AIM
To renew our vision of God's unending love for the world and to accept the challenges this makes to us.

Keynote readings
Isaiah 11.1-10
Isaiah 35.1-10
Malachi 3.1-5
Matthew 3.1-12
Romans 1.1-17

Way in
As individuals make a list of the enduring aspects of your lives (this might even include some possessions). Share some of them as a group. Then together make a list of enduring aspects from your community and the world at large. Why do you think they have lasted?

Faith
Read Romans 1.1-17.
- What inspired Paul to write these words and gave him such confidence in the gospel?
- Reflect on the significance of verses 16-17 for the approaching new Millennium.
- The basic gospel is the same, but how are we to share it with today's generation of young people to whom Church language is meaningless?

Hope
I believe that behind the mist the sun waits.
I believe that beyond the dark night it is raining stars.
I believe in secret volcanoes and the world below.
I believe that this lost ship will reach port.
They will not rob me of hope, it shall not be broken ...
My voice is filled to overflowing
with the desire to sing, the desire to sing.
I believe in reason, and not in force of arms;
I believe in our nobility, created in the image of God,
and with free will reaching for the skies.
They will not rob me of hope, it shall not be broken,
it shall not be broken.
From Chile
From Confessing our Faith Around the World
(World Council of Churches)

They will not rob me of hope

Most Latin American countries have returned to civilian rule after the oppression of years of military dictatorship. But economic inequality and injustice, with which the poor have lived for so long, are still rife. Yet hope persists. The Churches especially are committed to a spirituality

that enables people to find and support one another, gives strength to resist, to build community ...
- Share other stories which are familiar to you from around the world where hope sustains people in impossible circumstances.
- Are there other situations closer to you where you know the same to be true?
- What can we learn from the sense of hope expressed in the meditation on page 123?

Read Isaiah 11.1-10. These words were written in days of political insecurity, famine and gross economic inequalities. How do they challenge us as we approach the new Millennium?

Love
'God so loved the world ...' Reflect on God's love for the world – its peoples and their many cultures, its nations and governments, the world's amazing potential, majesty and splendour, fragility and pain, natural resources and wildlife ... When has our vision of God's world become too narrow? our awareness of God's love too personal?

Read Isaiah 35.1-10. In the light of your reflections on the universal love of God, what does it say to us? Think of other well-known prophecies we read at Christmas.

Read Malachi 3.1-5. Apart from the way tradition has linked these words with John the Baptist, the prophet challenges his contemporaries to look beyond religious formality to a wider vision of justice and mercy in society and the world. What are the challenges to the Church today?

Look again at the lists you made (at the beginning of the session) of things which have endured in your experience.
- Which of them matter most?
- What would you add to your list in the light of this discussion?
- Why did Paul say (1 Corinthians 13.13) that faith, hope and love endure?

Why did Paul say that faith, hope and love endure?

PRAYER

O Lord our God,
we thank you for the many people throughout the ages
who have followed your way of life joyfully:
for the many saints and martyrs, men and women,
who have offered up their very lives,
so that your life abundant may become manifest.
For your love and faithfulness we will at all times praise you.

O Lord, we thank you for those who chose the way of Jesus Christ.
In the midst of trial, they held out hope;
in the midst of hatred, they kindled love;
in the midst of persecutions, they witnessed to your power;
in the midst of despair, they clung to your promise.
For your love and faithfulness we will at all times praise you.

O Lord, we thank you for the truth they passed on to us:
that it is by giving that we shall receive;
it is by becoming weak that we shall be strong;
it is by loving others that we shall be loved;
it is by offering ourselves that the kingdom will unfold;
it is by dying that we shall inherit life everlasting.
Lord, give us courage to follow your way of life.
For your love and faithfulness we will at all times praise you.

From the 14th Biennial Convention Worship Book 1989
National Council of Churches of the Philippines

Study 3 *The way of obedience*

AIM

To be spiritually renewed as we look at the biblical emphasis on obedience.

Way in

1. What does the word 'obedience' call to mind? Brainstorm for a few minutes.
2. Ask the group to list occasions when Jesus spoke of, or demonstrated obedience. How far are we in danger of ignoring this emphasis?

Keynote readings
Amos 7.10-17
Luke 3.10-14
Matthew 11.2-15
Matthew 1.18-25
Luke 1.26-38
Luke 14.25-33

Challenge
Read Luke 3.10-14.
- What challenge does John the Baptist make to your community?
- Why do you think Jesus called him the greatest of the prophets? See Matthew 11.2-15.

The struggle
Read Luke 1.26-38.
- Why has Church tradition focused so much on the obedience of Mary the mother of Jesus?
- What is the difference between obedience and submission?

Notice how Mary's obedience brought her into conflict with cultural taboos, for who would believe her story of an angelic messenger and a virgin birth? She would be ostracized by her community. God's ways are not our ways.
- Where do you see God's ways conflicting with well-respected ways today? Think of examples.
- Where are we challenged to pay a high social price?
- And what about the call to repentance?

Conclude your discussion by reading Luke 14.25-33.

Where do you see God's ways conflicting with well-respected ways today?

PRAYER

For the darkness of waiting
 of not knowing what is to come
 of staying ready and quiet and attentive,
  we praise you O God:
   *For the darkness and the light
   are both alike to you.*

For the darkness of staying silent
 for the terror of having nothing to say
 and for the greater terror
 of needing to say nothing,
  we praise you O God:
   *For the darkness and the light
   are both alike to you.*

For the darkness of loving
in which it is safe to surrender
to let go of our self-protection
and to stop holding back our desire,
we praise you O God:
For the darkness and the light
are both alike to you.

For the darkness of choosing
when you give us the moment
to speak, and act, and change,
and we cannot know what we have
set in motion,
but we still have to take the risk,
we praise you O God:
For the darkness and the light
are both alike to you.

For the darkness of hoping
in a world which longs for you,
for the wrestling and the labouring of all creation
for wholeness and justice and freedom,
we praise you O God:
For the darkness and the light
are both alike to you.

Janet Morley
All Desires Known (SPCK)

ACTION

Pack up a food parcel and give it to someone who is homeless and in need.

INTERNATIONAL BIBLE READING ASSOCIATION

– a worldwide service of the National Christian Education Council at work in five continents.

HEADQUARTERS

1020 Bristol Road
Selly Oak
Birmingham
Great Britain
B29 6LB

and the following agencies

AUSTRALIA

The Joint Board of Christian Education
PO Box 1245 (65 Oxford Street)
Collingwood
Victoria 3066

GHANA

IBRA Secretary
PO Box 919
Accra

INDIA

All India Sunday School Association
PO Box 2099
Secunderabad – 500 003
Andhra Pradesh

NEW ZEALAND

Epworth Bookshop
PO Box 6133, Te Aro
75 Taranaki Street
Wellington 6035

NIGERIA

IBRA Representative
PMB 5298
Ibadan

SOUTH AND CENTRAL AFRICA

IBRA Representative
Box 9626
Edenglen 1613
Johannesburg